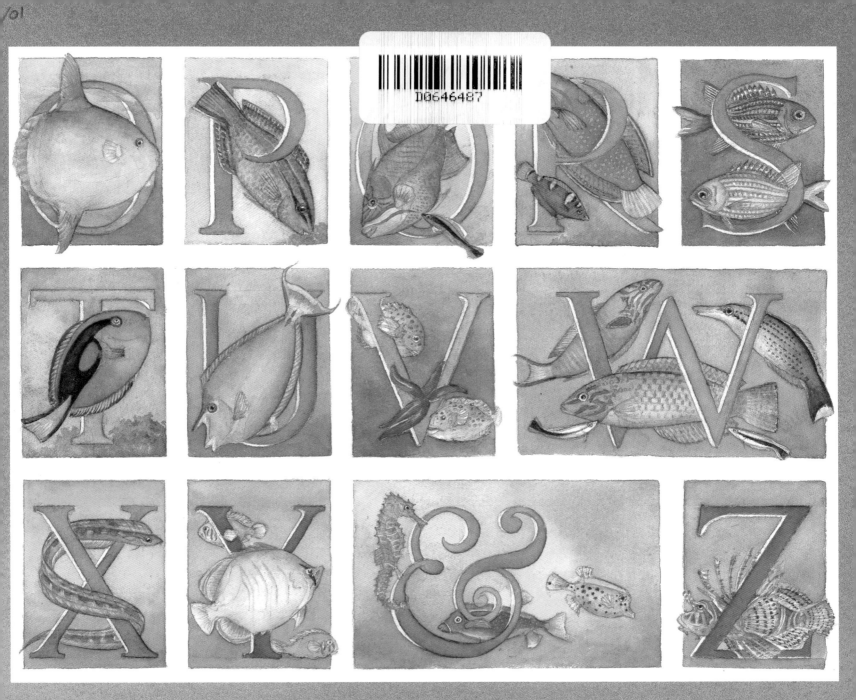

THE SECRET LIFE OF FISHES

From Angels to Zebras on the Coral Reef

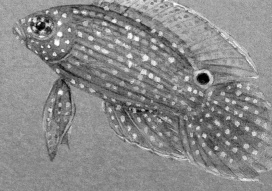

HARRY N. ABRAMS, INC., PUBLISHERS

THE SECRET LIFE OF FISHES
FROM ANGELS TO ZEBRAS ON THE CORAL REEF

WATERCOLORS & TEXT BY HELEN BUTTFIELD

Project Manager: Ruth A. Peltason
Editor: Julia Gaviria
Designers: Helen Buttfield, Miko McGinty

Library of Congress Cataloging-in-Publication Data
Buttfield, Helen.
The secret life of fishes : from angels to zebras
on the coral reef / watercolors and text
by Helen Buttfield.
p.   cm.
ISBN 0–8109–3933–9
1. Coral reef fishes. 2. Coral reef fishes—Pictorial works. I. Title.
QL620 .B88 1999
597.177'89—dc21   99–10892

Printed and bound in Hong Kong

Harry N. Abrams, Inc.
100 Fifth Avenue
New York, N.Y. 10011
www.abramsbooks.com

FISH IDENTIFICATIONS
Half-title page: Peppermint Angelfish, Zebra Lionfish
Title page: Vanderbilt's Chromis, Comet or Marine Betta, McCosker's
Flasher Wrasse courting females, Black-spot Pygmy Angelfish
Copyright page: Blue Triggerfish, Spikefin Goby, Leopard Blenny
Dedication: Titan Triggerfish, Bridled Parrotfish & juvenile, Bicolor Anthias
Table of Contents: Flame Angelfish, Beaked Coralfish, Tomato Clownfish,
Hector's Goby, Hawai'ian Longfin Anthias, Orange-tailed Leatherjacket,
Long-arm Octopus, Bicolor Parrotfish juvenile, Breastspot Cleaner Wrasse,
Three-lined Wrasse in initial phase being cleaned by a Southern Tubelip
juvenile, Reticulated Wrasse in initial phase, Green Ghost Pipefish,
Thornback Cowfish spawning, Starry Pufferfish juvenile
Acknowledgments: Yellow Seahorse

to Daniel Selznick & Richard Lewis

Nature's imagination is richer than our own.

— Freeman Dyson

CONTENTS

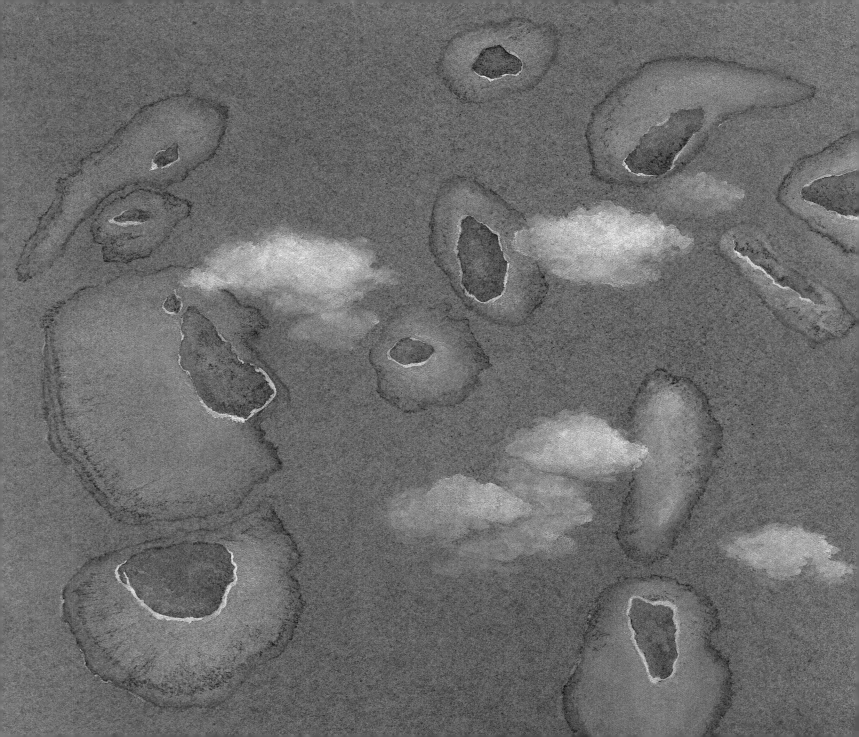

THE CORAL REEF is an underwater world of staggering diversity and abundance of life, the most densely populated habitat in the sea. Here, living together in an immense and complex web of relationships built up over millions of years of evolution, are creatures from every major branch of the animal and plant kingdoms. Many of the planet's life forms, snuffed out on land, are still represented in the warm, sunlit waters of tropical coral reefs. Nowhere else is there a world so transparent, so accessible, so open to observation and to wonder. It is also astonishingly beautiful, a realm of fantastic shapes, brilliant colors, shimmering light and movement.

Coral reefs are found in a belt encircling the globe between the tropics of Cancer and Capricorn, 23.5° north and south of the equator—and even farther where warm ocean currents keep the water temperature above 18°C. There are barrier reefs along the edges of continents, fringing reefs around tropical islands, and coral atolls surrounding lagoons where ancient volcanoes sank beneath the sea. The Great Barrier Reef, which extends for 1,400 miles along the eastern coast of Australia, is so massive that it can be seen from space. It is the largest organic structure on the planet, dwarfing anything made by man, yet it was built by unimaginable numbers of tiny colonial animals, coral polyps, over millions of years. Living symbiotically with *zooxanthellae*, microscopic plants that produce food by photosynthesis, the polyps secrete a stony skeleton, which forms the hard, enduring body of the reef. On this structure, an island of life in the vast ocean, countless floating larvae find a surface to attach themselves to grow and reproduce, creating brilliant gardens of soft corals, sponges, anemones, and other plantlike animals. Thousands of fish species, their larvae often carried hundreds of miles by the ocean currents, find food and shelter here. They swarm over the reef, singly, in pairs, or in glittering shoals, taking refuge from predators in its caves and crevices, feeding on the creatures supported by the reef, and even on the coral itself.

This is the home of the fishes in this book. Together with many invertebrates—bulldozing shrimp, boxing crabs, and deadly sea stars—their lives tell an extraordinary story. It is a tale of ruthless competition for space, for food, and for a chance to reproduce. But in this Darwinian struggle for survival there are many surprising forms of cooperation, beneficial alliances between fish and fish, or between fish and their invertebrate companions. They make up but one chapter in the fascinating story of the lives of the fishes on the coral reefs.

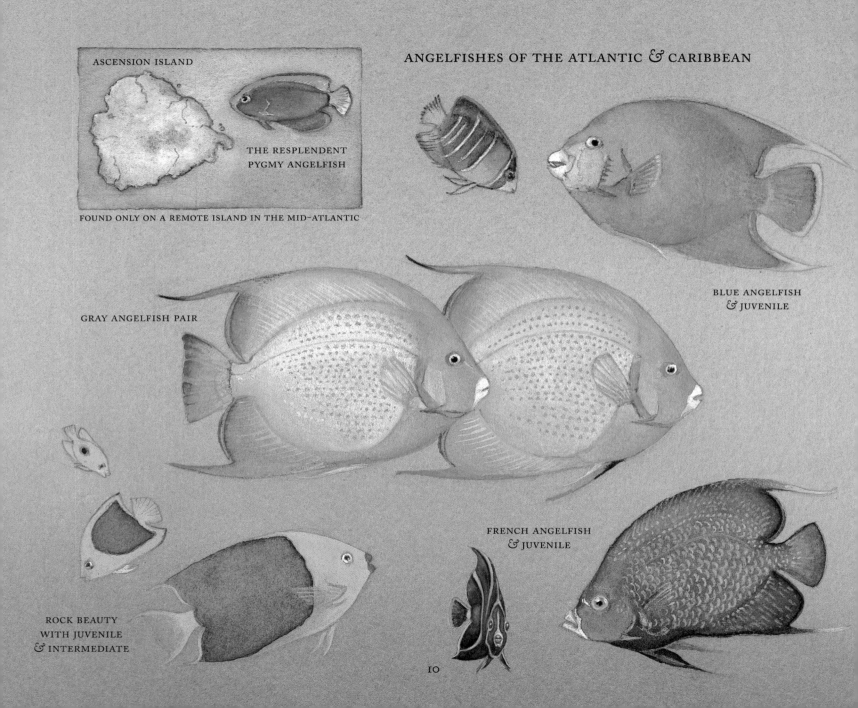

ASCENSION ISLAND

THE RESPLENDENT
PYGMY ANGELFISH

FOUND ONLY ON A REMOTE ISLAND IN THE MID-ATLANTIC

ANGELFISHES OF THE ATLANTIC & CARIBBEAN

BLUE ANGELFISH
& JUVENILE

GRAY ANGELFISH PAIR

FRENCH ANGELFISH
& JUVENILE

ROCK BEAUTY
WITH JUVENILE
& INTERMEDIATE

NGELFISH are the aristocrats of the coral reef. In their elegant costumes of dots, stripes, and masks of glowing color, they float effortlessly through the crowds of fishes, strange and beautiful. In one of the most intensely populated and colorful environments on earth, what is all this splendor for? Life on the reef is very much like life on land. There is intense competition to find a home, to mate and to reproduce, to eat, and above all, to avoid being eaten. In many ways that have only recently been observed, the fishes' brilliant colors serve them well.

Angelfish are grazers; alone or in pairs they cruise the reef face plucking the coral polyps and tiny crustaceans hiding in the crevices. The disruptive color patterns of the Pacific **Yellowmask Angelfish** break up its body outline against the brilliant corals, yet these same "poster colors" enable one angelfish to identify another quickly, distinguishing their mates from other angels. They also function as territorial markings that are recognized as "no trespassing" signs, preventing crowding and overgrazing.

Emperor Angelfish juveniles are so different from the territorial adults that the younger fishes are not seen as their competitors, and so are not driven away. As they grow, their markings are replaced by adult patterns and they must move off to find new territories, to mate, and to reproduce. Angels' courtship is very secret and is rarely seen. But the **Japanese Pygmy Angelfish,** in a prelude to spawning, will rapidly circle a female, soar above her, and then stop, all fins extended, in an underwater *grand jeté*.

ANTHIAS, sometimes called Lyre-tail Coralfish or Fairy Basslets, are small, exquisitely colored fish that live in colonies of hundreds, even thousands, on outer reef slopes from the Pacific Ocean to the Red Sea. Hovering within inches of the coral branches, they feed on plankton swept by on the current, and dive instantly to cover when alarmed. Unlike fish that commute daily between their coral homes and distant feeding grounds, Anthias are relatively safe from the dawn and dusk predators who lurk at the reef edges.

Anthias have evolved a communal society also found among animals and humans: the harem. But in these underwater harems *all* the members were once female. Only when they mature do some of the juveniles become males, with a few becoming the much larger and darker supermales with spectacular eye markings and filamentous fins. Each supermale reigns over twenty or more females, and tolerates only a few ordinary males. He spends most of his time defending his territory against rivals and in nightly mating rituals. With little time to eat or rest he does not live long. On his death the top-ranking female changes color and sex to take over his role.

The courting dance begins at dusk, with the supermale performing complex acrobatic displays for the entire colony. He swims upward in great circles, and drops down in long loops to climb even higher, stimulating the whole population to follow. The dance culminates in one or more pairings as the supermale and female swim side by side releasing eggs and sperm simultaneously into the current. As darkness falls they all retire to the reef for the night.

ASSLETS, especially **Fairy Basslets**, are often confused with Anthias, but they belong to two distinct families living on opposite sides of the globe—Anthias in the Pacific and Fairy Basslets or "Grammas" in the Atlantic. They are just as spectacularly colored as Anthias, but their lives are quite different. Shy and secretive, Fairy Basslets are solitary dwellers in the maze of coral, defending territories against other basslets, the males fighting fiercely at mating time.

The neutral buoyancy provided by their air-filled swim bladders enable these tiny fish to hover in any position, floating like astronauts in space, usually oriented to the nearest surface. **Royal Grammas,** browsing over coral heads or fighting for territory, swim right side up. A **Blackcap Gramma** (above), feeding in a cave, swims upside down.

Batfish are giants in comparison to basslets. Although juveniles are only inches long, they grow to almost two feet. Drifting slowly and majestically in the current, adults feed on algae, plankton, and invertebrates. Young fish survive by mimicking floating leaves, so as not to be eaten by larger fish. The coral reef is a great city in the vast ocean, and like cities on land it has its sharks—and the Barracuda.

Barracuda are voracious predators, but they are so narrow that from the front they are almost invisible. A solitary barracuda is like a shadow, unseen until it strikes. In packs they are a terrifying phalanx of hunters that scatters schools of fish, picking them off one by one. Some say that when sated, Barracuda will herd fish into the shallows to eat later.

BLENNIES are small fish, only a few inches long, and they are both lurkers and darters. Some are quite drab, blending into rock and tide pools; others living on the open reef have colors that match the brilliance of the corals. They usually lie hidden in corals or sponges, propped up on their slender pelvic fins, eagerly scanning the sea for the planktonic crustaceans on which they feed. Many have weedlike or feathery appendages growing from their heads that camouflage them in seaweed.

The agile rock blennies respond to the tides by climbing up on rocks at low tide and dropping back into the water when the tide returns, dashing about feeding and chasing one another. They use their strong pectoral fins to propel themselves through the shallows and even across the rocks. The splendid male **Longhorn Blenny** selects a nest and attracts the female by doing push-ups on his pelvic fins and by bumping against her with his nose. The female enters the nest tail first and deposits her eggs, which are then fertilized by the male. She swims off and the male remains to guard the eggs, for many other fishes find them an easy, nourishing meal.

The eyes of the **Downy Blenny** move independently as she peers intently from her hole, giving her the appearance of being a very smart fish. In fact, the little blenny *is* one of the most intelligent of fishes. Scientists have taught blennies to tell objects apart by their color, shape, or size, and even to read distinctions between certain letters of the alphabet, such as U and E or W and L.

A blenny of another stripe is the **Bluelined Sabretooth** (top), guarding his nest of eggs laid by the female in an empty shell. He mimics both the appearance *and* the swimming movements of the trusted Cleaner Wrasse, but instead of cleaning other fishes this imposter dashes out to nip morsels from their fins.

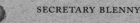

SECRETARY BLENNY

BUTTERFLYFISH, closely related to Angelfish, are among the most numerous of the coral reef fishes, with over a hundred species. Their flattened, dislike shape lets them move quickly and easily around the coral heads, swimming with a rowing motion of their pectoral fins. It also enables them to remain vertically stable at slow speeds while feeding in the intricate maze of branching corals, sea fans, and sponges. Their small, protractile mouths and many fine, sharp teeth (which give them the name *chaetodon,* the brush-toothed) are well adapted for coral browsing. The dazzling pattern of dots and dashes creates optical illusions that distract and confuse their predators. Many, like the **Fourspot Butterflyfish,** have false eyespots near the tail; the real eye is camouflaged, usually by a dark stripe. A predator preparing to strike anticipates forward movement and often completely misses the head, striking harmlessly at the tail. Butterflyfish are rarely found in the stomachs of predators.

Crown Butterflyfish often swim in pairs, feeding on coral polyps, tube worms, and small invertebrates. Once they have formed this lasting bond, they rarely stray far apart. They have excellent eyesight and appear to keep close track of each other while feeding. Should they become separated one will often swim to the top of the nearest coral head and hover conspicuously there. Its mate soon appears, flashing its patterned side as a sign of recognition.

All butterflyfish are diurnal, feeding by day and resting by night in their favorite hiding places in the reef. Many species can change color, fading or darkening their bodies to blend more closely with the shadows. Do they sleep? Like most fishes they do, entering a state of torpor throughout the night. The rare and beautiful **Triangular Butterflyfish** almost disappears in the shadowy darkness.

CARDINALFISH are small fishes, often a brilliant scarlet resembling the cloaks of the ecclesiastical cardinals whose name they bear. Like all cardinalfish, **Flamefish** are nocturnal, hiding in the reef by day and emerging only after dark to feed on zooplankton and small crustaceans. Their large eyes give them excellent night vision, and their red color, which appears black, hides them from the many hungry predators who roam the reef at night. When alarmed they dive into crevices or even into the waving arms of an anemone, carefully avoiding the tentacles, for they are not immune to its venomous sting. **Yellow-lined Cardinalfish** (right) have taken brief refuge in the spines of a *Diadema* sea urchin. Another cardinal species lives within the red sea urchin, which parts its spines to allow them to enter; the fish reciprocates by cleaning the urchin's skin. This symbiotic behavior, in which both sides benefit from their intimate association, is called mutualism. It plays a vital role on the reef, helping many of its most vulnerable creatures survive.

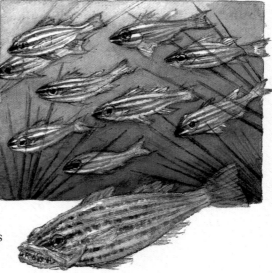

Most cardinalfish are mouth brooders: the male incubates the eggs in his mouth, constantly turning them about to keep them aerated. **Eight-lined Cardinalfish** carry their defenseless hatchlings for up to two weeks, greatly increasing their chances in life. **Pajama Cardinalfish** sport a two-piece pattern that breaks up their body outline making them hard for predators to see, but easy for the Pajamas to recognize each other. The smallest, and most security conscious of all, is the **Conchfish.** Locked by day in the dark mantle cavity of the **Queen Conch,** 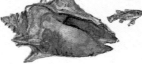 it emerges at night to feed on tiny crustaceans.

CROAKERS or Drums are some of the noisiest fishes in the sea. Their croaking or drumming is made by vibrating muscles attached to the swim bladder, which amplifies the sound, making it so loud that it can be heard above water. The juvenile **Cubbyu** will lose their long dorsal fins and stripes as they grow, but not their drums.

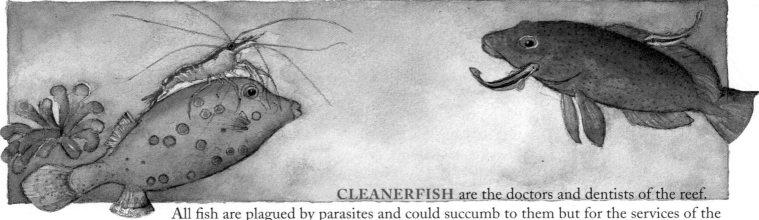

CLEANERFISH are the doctors and dentists of the reef. All fish are plagued by parasites and could succumb to them but for the services of the cleaners. At cleaning stations near prominent corals or sponges, they run "swim-in clinics" where fishes gather in groups to wait for treatment. Some cleaners, like this Pacific **Cleaner Shrimp** grooming a **Cube Boxfish** (left), work alone, but others, like the brightly striped **Cleaning Gobies**, run a group practice, with a number of fish working on each client, here (above right) a Caribbean **Coney**. Even the fiercest carnivores allow these small fish to approach without harm, docilely opening their mouths to have their teeth scraped and their gills cleaned.

A little **Boxer Crab** is much less trusting. stinging anemones and carries them about  Lacking powerful claws, he picks up small like boxing gloves to ward off predators.

DAMSELFISH have been called the sparrows of the sea. Hovering over the coral heads in great shining shoals, they dart and swoop together, snapping up the plankton. Using their pectoral fins like oars, they propel themselves forward with great speed and agility, disappearing into the reef instantly when a shadow passes overhead. In these damsel shoals each fish reacts on its own, for unlike polarized schools that swim in tight formation, shoals are loose aggregations of fishes that share the same instincts, feeding habits, and territories. At dusk, clouds of iridescent **Blue-green Chromis** descend like birds to the reef to shelter for the night in dense swarms beneath ledges and in caves, their brilliant blue-green fading to a dusky blue-gray.

In spite of their gentle name and modest size, damselfish are the most pugnacious of all the territorial fishes, especially at mating time. After the eggs are laid the male takes up watch over them. He swims back and forth, both to aerate the eggs and to defend them against predators, which are often other male damselfish. But he will fearlessly attack *any* intruder, even one many times his size. If a diver comes too close to a nest, a fierce little fish no bigger than his thumb rushes out to defend it, nipping at arms or fingers.

Clownfish or **Anemonefish** are damselfish that live within the stinging tentacles of a venomous anemone whose touch instantly paralyzes other small fishes. The anemone offers a safe refuge for the fish, who snuggles within its soft tentacles, completely oblivious to their deadly sting. But each clownfish must slowly habituate its host to his presence before he will become immune, gradually coating his scales with the slime that protects him from their sting. Clownfish rarely stray from the safety of their anemone homes for there they can feed, sleep, find mates, and even build nests.

MOST DAMSELFISH guard and tend their eggs, but once hatched the little fish are on their own. An exception is the **Spiny Chromis,** or **Spottytail Humbug,** a species remarkable in coral reef society for the care of their young. Pairing up for a four-month breeding season, the male and female prepare a well-hidden nest that they tend together, where they clean and guard the eggs. But instead of abandoning the young fish to the uncertainties of planktonic life, as do most reef fishes, these feisty parents keep their brood of a hundred or more schooled tightly about them, chasing away all predators. The juveniles eventually wander off, mixing with the young of neighboring groups. This increased protection is clearly a favorable evolutionary adaptation for the Spiny Chromis is one of the most abundant of all Pacific damselfish.

Another member of this successful family is the **Three-spot Damselfish** found on many Caribbean islands. This enterprising fish is a farmer, cultivating algae that grow on **Staghorn** and **Star Corals.** Each three-spot tends a small algal plot a square foot or more, vigorously defending his crop against all comers. He must constantly patrol his territory, chasing off damsel neighbors as well as other much larger algae eaters: wrasses, triggerfishes, and the destructive herds of coral-crunching parrotfish.

Three-spots get little rest. At night hordes of sea urchins creep relentlessly over the coral like armored tanks, digesting the algae as they pass. These voracious coral grazers, bristling with spines, must be carried off. If an urchin is too large to move, a three-spot will nip off its spines, one by one. They are truly indomitable fish. Living in colonies, each guards its own farm, but close to others, their combined defenses provide greater protection for all.

19

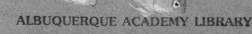

ELS swim like snakes but in three dimensions. A **Chain Moray** (swimming above) undulates the whole length of his body, generating a backward thrust against the water, which drives him forward. This also increases drag, however, making him a slower, less efficient swimmer. But eels do not need to be fast. They hunt by stealth, hiding their long bodies, often with over a hundred vertebrae, in holes in the reef, where they lie in wait for passing fish and crustaceans. The beautiful **Blue-ribbon Eel** is so fierce and deadly that it has no need for protective coloration. Although juveniles are a cryptic black, the adults are brilliant blue and yellow. Leafy, yellow nose flaps act as a lure to entice small fishes within reach of this male's sharp-toothed jaws. Unlike other morays, when the jaws snap shut he coils *backward* into his hole. The **Goldentail Moray** (right), whose open jaws display a set of needlelike teeth, seems fierce but is really quite shy. His menacing gape is not a threat but a necessity. The open jaws keep water flowing over his gills, allowing him to breathe, while his exquisite sense of smell picks up the scent of distant prey carried in the water.

Conger Eels are round-bodied eels whose long fins form a continuous fringe around their tails. **Spotted Garden Eels** are congers that are completely sedentary: rooted in the sea bottom in large colonies, they wave around like plants, feeding on plankton carried by the current. They rarely leave their holes; even when mating they leave their tails firmly anchored in the sand. The slender **Spotted Snake Eels** have muscular bodies with strong spikelike tails with which they burrow into the bottom, where they move about, swimming rather swiftly under the sand.

MPERORS have large heads and big mouths, thick lips, and a formidable set of teeth. The massive molars of **Bigeye Emperors** enable them to easily crack open hard-shelled invertebrates such as crabs and mollusks, and even to crunch through the terrible sharp spines of the sea urchin. With their large eyes they can see clearly in the dark to hunt the red urchins that creep over the reef surfaces. To elude the larger night predators that feed on them Bigeyes can turn their dark patterns on and off, and their small mottled juveniles hide easily behind rocks or in coral crevices.

The large, red **Trumpet Emperor** has a long, sloping snout with many sharp, conical teeth with which he seizes the small fish that make up his diet. He is a voracious nocturnal hunter, but will snap up any unlucky fish that crosses his path by day. In turn he is himself the prize catch of the greatest predator of all, man.

Like all reef dwellers, **Golden-lined Emperors** are linked not only to the cycle of day and night, but to the tides and to the moon which governs them. During the first five nights of the lunar month large groups of these emperors gather to spawn on the outer edges of many Pacific islands, releasing eggs and sperm when the highest tides will carry them safely out to sea.

FUSILIERS, with their long tapered bodies and deeply forked tails, are swift and agile swimmers. They congregate by day in immense schools, patrolling the reef face to feed on planktonic plants and animals, many the larval young of fishes that live on the reef. Fusiliers are preyed upon by larger fish, but are protected by their numbers, each school a superorganism of hundreds of individuals, argus-eyed, dodging and turning in perfect unison. This swirling mass makes a confusing target for predators: a few fish may be eaten, but the rest survive.

Filefish have evolved a very different strategy. Most are elaborately patterned and colored so that when swimming among the corals, undulating only the dorsal and anal fins, they are almost invisible. **Longnose Filefish** (above) often feed in pairs, using their extended snouts and tiny mouths to graze on the polyps of *Acropora* coral or on tiny invertebrates hidden in crevices. The portly **Mimic Filefish** (far left) has a cunning disguise: he wears the distinctive spotted suit of the **Saddleback Puffer,** which is too poisonous to eat. Only his fins give him away.

All filefish are skilled in camouflage. Reclusive and secretive, they hide among corals and sea fans, changing pattern and color to match their surroundings. Bristly hairs on the scales give their skin its filelike texture, and they can erect their long, first dorsal spines to intimidate their rivals, to jam themselves firmly into holes, or to block a predator's throat. Filefish also make sharp sounds called stridulations by rubbing together spines in their fins. The solitary Micronesian **Wirenet Filefish** sometimes sounds like a great underwater cricket.

Of all the seven flatfish families superbly adapted to life on the bottom, flounders are certainly the most beautiful. They begin life as floating larvae with normal eyes, but as they develop, one eye gradually migrates over the top of the head to the other side, allowing the pancake-thin adult to rest invisibly on its pale blindside. Its upper surface is patterned with sensitive color cells called *chromophores,* which expand and contract, rapidly varying color and pattern to match the background. The **Panther Flounder** (above) is clearly visible while swimming, but melts against the sand as soon as he rests on the bottom. Even **Peacock Flounders,** with their elegant blue rosettes, seem to disappear when they settle, their color fading as they swish their fins to cover themselves with sand. Motionless but alert, flounders are keen ambush hunters, as their eyes on mobile stalks can move independently, scanning the water for small fish and other crustaceans that venture too close.

The master of camouflage is the **Giant Frogfish,** one of the Anglerfish mob, a voracious carnivore, and leading candidate for Fastest Gun on the Reef. So closely do they mimic the appearance of algae-covered rocks or colorful sponges that many divers, like many unlucky fish, never even see them. The first dorsal spine is modified as a long fishing pole with a wormlike "lure" on the end. Any hungry little fish moving in to investigate is

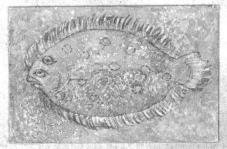

instantly inhaled by the suction created when the frogfish opens his great mouth. This vanishing act, invisible to the human eye, has been timed at 1/100th of a second!

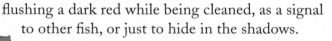

GOATFISH are predators of the sandy bottoms, whose fleshy chin barbels are a cross between whiskers and sensitive fingers. With special cells that function as taste buds, Goatfish use their barbels to probe the sand or coral rubble, searching out small worms and crustaceans. The fishes tuck their barbels under gill covers when swimming, and courting males wiggle them at females. In the Red Sea clever **Bird Wrasse** often hunt with the **Forsskal's Goatfish**, their long snouts exploring crannies and probing deep in the sand. The two work together in tandem, each feeding better than he would alone. When alarmed or excited, goatfish can change colors in seconds, often flushing a dark red while being cleaned, as a signal to other fish, or just to hide in the shadows.

Goatfish are nocturnal, sheltering by day in mixed schools with fish like the **French Grunts.** At sunset they emerge in small groups and head toward the outer reef, where they gather and, like a convoy of ships, move off to the grass beds to feed. This mass schooling, often in the thousands, protects them during the dangerous twilight, when both day and night predators are abroad. Some grunts, when moved by scientists to unfamiliar reefs, at first wandered about in confusion. But in a few days they had learned from the local grunts how to find the safest migration routes to their new feeding grounds.

Many grunts, like the handsome **Porkfish,** make the sound that gives them their name by grinding pharyngeal teeth in the throat. Why they do this is a mystery.

GOBIES are miniature fish, some only an inch long, but they make up the largest family of fishes in the tropical seas. They are shown here at actual size: the reclusive **Rusty Goby** perched under the top of the letter G is barely an inch, the **Greenbanded Goby** peering out the bottom is not much bigger, and the **Galapagos Blue-banded Goby,** in dark glasses and striped suit, is only an inch and a quarter. The tiniest of all gobies, a freshwater species, is half an inch when fully grown; it is the smallest known vertebrate on land or sea. Such tasty mouthfuls spend most of their time hiding in the sand, in sponges, or in corals, like the **Maori Goby** above, darting out briefly to feed and mate. Most gobies, who have no buoyant swim bladders, rest easily on the bottom, their ventral fins often fused into a cupped disc to help hold them fast.

Many gobies have evolved symbiotic partnerships with other reef residents. A "lookout" goby, **Wheeler's Shrimp Goby,** lives with a blind shrimp, often called a bulldozer shrimp for his tireless efforts shoveling out the sand to maintain their burrow. The shrimp uses his antennae to remain in constant touch with the sharp-eyed goby, who can sense approaching predators by smell, as well as by sight. When alerted to danger he signals the shrimp by the flick of his tail and they both vanish into the burrow. Often a pair of gobies and a pair of shrimp share the same home, doubling their security.

The **Signal Goby** feeds on the fringes of the reef, gulping sand to sieve tiny crustaceans through its gills. False eyespots make it look like a crab scuttling sideways.

A FEW OF THE VARIATIONS IN COLOR, PATTERN & SIZE AMONG INDO-PACIFIC & AUSTRALIAN GROUPERS

RED-SPOTTED ROCK COD

CORONATION TROUT

HONEYCOMB COD

CORAL TROUT

POLKA-DOT CORAL TROUT

POTATO COD (OR POTATO GROUPER)

HIGH-FIN CORAL TROUT

CAMOUFLAGE GROUPER

PEACOCK GROUPER

BARRAMUNDI COD

SIX-BANDED ROCK COD

SCALE 1:10

ROUPERS belong to a large family, with almost 400 related species. The smallest is only two inches long, but others are as big as the humans diving among them—some much bigger. The Queensland Grouper is nine feet long and weighs eight hundred pounds. The largest of all bony reef fishes, it is twice the size of the **Potato Cod** (shown opposite). Stories of giant groupers inhaling divers in a single gulp are legendary; some even say that the "great fish" that swallowed Jonah was a grouper, not a whale! On Caribbean reefs **Nassau Groupers** (relatively modest at four feet and fifty pounds) are the hulking, friendly fish that feed from divers' hands and steal fish from their pockets. These solitary hunters hover near the bottom, waiting motionless to ambush any small fish that ventures too close. As the grouper opens its tremendous mouth the powerful suction, like a great vacuum cleaner, draws the fish into oblivion.

Groupers go through startling transformations. They can abruptly change their brilliant patterns and colors, altering them to match the background, and shed their stripes and bars, turning pale or darkening when alarmed. When fighting and courting, or when soliciting the services of cleanerfish, they often turn a dark red. A **Tiger Grouper** starts life as a yellow juvenile and only gradually develops the ten yellow-brown bars that help hide it from its prey in the dappled sunlight and shadows of the reef.

Some groupers also change sex as they grow. Starting as females they produce eggs; later as males they generate sperm. Yet others are hermaphroditic: simultaneously male and female, they can produce both sperm and eggs. By cross-fertilization they double the number of young, greatly increasing the species' chances of survival. There are many gorgeous groupers on the coral reefs of both the Atlantic and the Indo-Pacific oceans.

HAWKFISH, like their aerial namesakes, are superb predators, sharp-eyed, swift, and sure. They perch motionless on the outer branches of coral heads waiting to swoop down on passing fish and crustaceans. The **Tartan Hawkfish** relies on camouflage: its brilliant colors and patterns blend into the network of coral branches and sea fans. The smaller **Pixy Hawkfish** has a subtler strategy: as it raises and lowers its dorsal fins tiny filaments wriggle like worms, mimicking the coral polyps and luring hungry coral feeders. In a split second the eaters become the eaten—seized in the plierlike jaws, they disappear into the hawkfish stomach.

Humbugs, or **White-tailed Damselfish** (lurking behind the H above), are gentler fish. In colonies of hundreds, they hover over the coral, feeding on plankton. Unlike other damselfish they share their territories, but even as they retreat into coral niches they turn and raise their fins to display bold stripes that warn other fish to keep away.

Hamlets dress in a variety of colors and patterns—white, yellow, orange, blue, and brown, some spotted, some barred or striped—and in multiple combinations of these. One even wears a Shakespearean suit of solemn black. They were once thought to be color varieties of a single species, the **Butter Hamlet** (bottom left), but most scientists now believe they are separate species. They spawn prodigiously, often with other color forms, creating many beautiful hybrids. Each fish is hermaphroditic, both male and female, producing eggs *and* sperm; cross-fertilizing provides an effective survival strategy on a reef full of hungry mouths.

BUTTER HAMLET   GOLDEN HAMLET   SHY HAMLET   BARRED HAMLET

Above the outer edges of the coral reefs two long and slender predators hover just below the water surface: the **Halfbeak** and the **Houndfish**. Their bodies are countershaded: dark above, protecting them from the eyes of birds circling overhead, and pale underneath, making them invisible to prey or predators below. **Halfbeaks** are only about a foot long, but most of their length is an extended needle-sharp lower jaw, often tipped with red. They feed on anything that moves: bits of algae, seagrass, zooplankton, and hapless small fishes, like the **Dwarf Herring** (above). With lightning-swift movements, these flat-bellied, silvery fish skitter at the surface, often leaping over floating sticks and gliding in the air on outstretched pectoral fins, in pursuit of prey or to escape their own predators, or perhaps just for fun.

The **Houndfish** is formidable, often five feet long and armed with a pair of long pointed jaws studded with sharp teeth. His underbelly is white, his back is green—and so are his bones. It is not surprising that his species name is *crocodilus*. Preying on small plankton eaters, houndfish are themselves the prey of those at the top of the food chain: sharks and barracuda. They have been called "living javelins" by ocean fishermen, for at night they often leap from the water and hurtle through the air. It is a sorry fisherman who gets in their way.

BLUE HAMLET   INDIGO HAMLET   YELLOWTAIL HAMLET   BLACK HAMLET

DOL OF THE MOORS, the **Moorish Idol,** is generally considered one of the world's most beautiful fishes. Its pattern of black and white bars appears often on other reef fish such as the **Pennant Bannerfish** and the **Wimplefish** (often called the Poorman's Moorish Idol), and is clearly a highly effective defense—the black-and-white shapes are more apparent than the fishes. But the Moorish Idol is the most bizarre and elegant of them all. Triangular fins extend its wafer-thin body like curving brushstrokes, and a long filament rises from the enlarged dorsal spine. It has short horns above its eyes and a pointed nose with tweezerlike jaws to pluck small crustaceans from coral crevices. Its bold black-and-white pattern may seem to make it an easy target as it swims lazily along the reef—but only when seen from the side. With a quick flick of its fins and tail, this magical fish can turn in an instant. As the pattern disappears, so does the fish.

The Moorish Idol is found on almost every reef in the vast Pacific. How does it travel so far? Adults cannot leave the reefs, but their offspring can and do—in the millions. Their larvae can survive in the floating plankton for a hundred days, a record for reef fish. The great ocean currents sweeping across the Indo-Pacific have spread them from the Red Sea to the Galapagos

PENNANT BANNERFISH

WIMPLEFISH

MOORISH IDOL

JACKS are supersonic swimmers of the open ocean and outer reefs; their tapered bodies and powerful forked tails are built for acceleration. In the twilight of dawn and dusk—the commuter hour for many reef fish—they loom up from the depths to cruise the reef edges. Large eyes give jacks excellent vision, but in the dim light they rely on their lateral lines, canals and nerves that run along their sides and provide an additional sense: they can "hear" the vibrations sent through the water by the swimming movements of their prey.

Almaco Jacks are large, heavy-bodied fish up to three feet long, and are superb predators. They travel alone or in packs along the reef face, often ignored by their prey—but only until they begin to hunt. Zigzagging back and forth, they pick up speed, and the feeding fish, sensing danger, pack more closely together or quickly seek shelter. The jack strikes like lightning; even as the school splits and turns some fish are gone. The rest return to browsing—until the next strike.

The **Yellowhead Jawfish** is a small, slender fish with very large jaws. He digs a vertical burrow in the sandy bottom, fortifying it with bits of rubble and stone. Hovering nervously above his hole, he snatches plankton, small crustaceans, and fish from the water. When alarmed, he vanishes instantly into his hole—tail first. At night, like a good homeowner in dangerous territory, he covers the entrance with a small pebble or shell.

ŪPĪPĪ is the Hawai'ian name for the **Blackspot Sergeant,** a fish found on every coral reef in the Indo-Pacific. Evolutionary biologists believe that most reef fish probably originated in the Indo-Australian archipelago and have spread to other reefs, often across many hundreds of miles of open ocean. Although adult fish cannot survive such long distances, their larvae can. Some live up to ninety days drifting in the currents that circle the globe. Arriving at last on a coral reef, they settle down to grow and reproduce. Some species, like the **Kūpīpī,** remain the same for millennia. Others gradually change and new species evolve as genetic mutations prove advantageous in the struggle for survival in the new reef environment.

TINKER'S BUTTERFLYFISH

KIKĀKAPU

On remote islands, like the Galapagos or Hawai'i, favorable mutations quickly become established in the gene pool, causing species to evolve more rapidly. A quarter of all Hawai'ian fishes are endemics, species found nowhere else. Many of these are butterflyfishes, called **Kapuhili** by the Hawai'ians, that flourish on the reefs, often feeding on the coral polyps themselves. Other species, like the **Ornate Butterflyfish** or **Kikākapu,** with its beautiful gold stripes, are found on many other Pacific islands as well. **Tinker's Butterflyfish,** named after a renowned marine biologist, was long thought to be endemic, but has recently been found on other nearby islands.

RIGHT: *Captain Cook's map of the Sandwich or Hawai'ian Islands with fish endemic to Hawai'i or abundant there:* 1. *Milletseed or Lemon Butterflyfish* 2. *Multiband Butterflyfish* 3. *Bluestripe Butterflyfish* 4. *Fantail Filefish* 5. *Chocolate-dip Chromis* 6. *Potter's Angelfish* 7. *Bandit Angelfish* 8. *Yellow Tang (Hawai'i has its largest schools)* 9. *Reef or Picasso Triggerfish (Hawai'ian state fish: Humuhumu nukunuku a pua'a)* 10. *Regal Parrotfish* 11. *Flame Wrasse* 12. *Psychedelic Wrasse (male and female)* 13. *Blackside Razorfish (juvenile)*

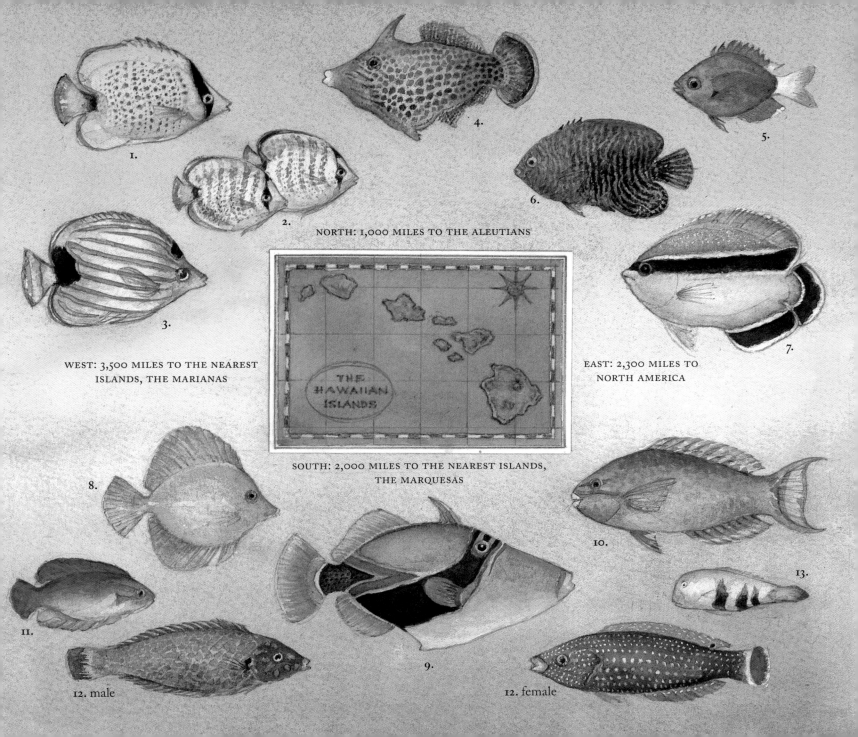

NORTH: 1,000 MILES TO THE ALEUTIANS

WEST: 3,500 MILES TO THE NEAREST
ISLANDS, THE MARIANAS

THE HAWAIIAN ISLANDS

EAST: 2,300 MILES TO
NORTH AMERICA

SOUTH: 2,000 MILES TO THE NEAREST ISLANDS,
THE MARQUESAS

1.

2.

3.

4.

5.

6.

7.

8.

9.

10.

11.

12. male

12. female

13.

LEATHERJACKET is the Australians' name for the rough-skinned filefish, and two-thirds of the known species inhabit their waters. Leatherjackets swim slowly, hardly bending their bodies, yet by undulating their dorsal fins and tail they can hover over the coral, tearing food from the surface and plucking invertebrates from crevices. The sharp spine above the forehead is a powerful deterrent to larger predators. The **Scribbled Leatherjacket**, feeding in the letter L, is found in all tropical seas; the **Horseshoe** and tiny **Pygmy Leatherjacket**, only on South Pacific and Australian reefs.

The astonishingly beautiful Lionfish is not much of a swimmer either. All dazzle and guile, it is also invulnerable, for its venomous spines inflict excruciating pain, and even death, on any creature that touches them. The **Peacock Lionfish** drifts through the water behind its fluttering ribbony fins, herding small fish into a corner to engulf them in its great maw. Many fishes are found in its stomach, but it rarely shows up in the stomachs of others.

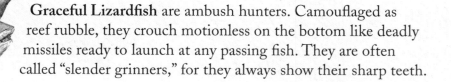

Graceful Lizardfish are ambush hunters. Camouflaged as reef rubble, they crouch motionless on the bottom like deadly missiles ready to launch at any passing fish. They are often called "slender grinners," for they always show their sharp teeth.

MORAYS & MANDARINFISH are among the largest and the smallest of the reef fishes. Morays can grow up to nine feet long; Mandarinfish are only two inches. Brilliantly colored and elaborately patterned, these little fish belong to a group called dragonets, or little dragons. The male is larger and more splendidly colored than the female, and his colors grow even brighter as he courts her, flashing his erect dorsal fin. The two release eggs and sperm simultaneously into the current that will carry the fertilized eggs away from the dangers of the reef.

Their sinister expressions and snakelike form have given **Morays** a bad reputation. If provoked they will certainly use their sharp teeth to defend themselves, but they pose little threat to careful divers, for to them we must seem much larger and more dangerous fish. Peering by day from their lairs in rock or coral caves, they emerge at night to roam the reef—swift and implacable hunters. Their keen sense of smell enables them to locate their prey in total darkness, and their long thin bodies can penetrate the narrowest spaces to reach hidden crabs or solitary sleeping fish. Few reef creatures can elude a determined moray.

But hunters need good teeth and these fierce predators become surprisingly docile when visiting the dentist. Approaching a cleaning station the **Tropical** or **Pearly Moray** hovers motionless, opening its terrible jaws to have its teeth scraped and parasites removed. When its patience is exhausted, it shakes its body or snaps its jaws and the cleaner wrasses depart—in a hurry.

ANTA RAYS are majestic wanderers of tropical oceans, giants among the fishes. They are superbly adapted to life in the open sea. Shaped like a huge kite, the manta's flattened body and large, triangular pectoral fins form a winged disc whose aerodynamic contour offers little resistance to the water. Slow, powerful strokes of its fin tips propel it effortlessly forward and provide the lift that keeps it aloft, for mantas, like sharks and other cartilaginous fishes, have no swim bladders to maintain buoyancy. They must swim or glide almost constantly, and as they swim they feed. Their cephalic lobes, two long, spiraling flaps on either side of the head, channel a stream of water into the manta's wide mouth, sending vital oxygen to the gills, where rows of gill rakers strain out the microscopic plankton and small fishes destined for the manta's stomach. A manta with a twelve-foot wingspan weighs over a ton and is the size of a small Volkswagen, but like most large fishes, mantas feed on the smallest of creatures living at the bottom of the food chain, for only their vast numbers can provide enough nourishment to feed the manta's bulk.

The plankton-rich waters off coral reefs provide a feast for mantas, who gather there in great numbers, soaring in the currents that sweep through the passes. Here they also find many cleanerfishes, who are eager to rid the mantas of parasites while acquiring a meal for themselves. As a Pacific manta approaches the reef a **Clarion Angelfish** swims out to graze on the manta's body, a banquet table for the eight-inch angelfish. Another guest of the manta is a free-swimming **Remora** hitching a ride on the manta's back, attached upside down by a suckered plate on the top of its head. It employs the manta as a mobile base from which to feed.

Mantas are powerful swimmers and amazing acrobats. They can leap up to five feet out of the water, emerging headfirst to revolve in a slow, breathtaking cartwheel before falling back into the sea. One pregnant female, on being harpooned, dropped her single pup in midair. Opening its folded pectoral fins it turned, dove into the sea, and swam away.

The **Marine Betta**, or **Comet** (who also appears on the title page), is a beautiful
spotted fish, but a timid one. Alarmed by the shadows passing overhead, it
dives headfirst into a small coral crevice, as if it knew that its protruding tail
and white-rimmed eyespot mimic the head of a **Whitemouth Moray**
(opposite), an eel sure to intimidate almost all its predators.

EEDLEFISH are perfectly named both for their slender needlelike bodies and their needle-sharp teeth. They congregate in huge schools above the reef and drift just below the waves to dart at devastating speed after small fish schooling near the surface. They can rely on stealth as well as speed, for from the front their small heads and narrow bodies are hardly visible. Their fins, set like the feathers of an arrow, keep the **Reef Needlefish** on target; their long jaws and sharp teeth seize and hold their slippery prey. A quick flip sends the hapless fish sliding straight down into the long needlefish stomach.

The **Chambered Nautilus** is one of the oldest creatures in the sea, dating back 180 million years. It is the only remnant of a group of over two thousand giant species that once filled the great world ocean. Like octopus and cuttlefish they are not fishes but *cephalopods* (head-footers), invertebrates whose body plan is one of the most successful ever evolved. The nautilus actually has no body to speak of: its eighty or ninety tentacles grow directly out of the head, well positioned to seize food and put it directly into the sharp parrotlike beak.

Deep ridges on its tentacles provide the nautilus with powerful suction that holds its prey in a viselike grip; it can also use them to grapple to a rock or reef wall when threatened, presenting its impregnable shell to any predator. The nautilus secretes this shell, adding new chambers in a spiral as its grows, and fills them with gas whose volume the nautilus adjusts to rise or sink at will. It rests in deep water during the day and rises to the reef at night to feed on crabs and small shellfish, propelling itself in any direction by moving a flexible siphon lodged among the tentacles. The primitive eye has no lens and so functions much like a pinhole camera, but the nautilus has very little need to see, for chemical receptors in its tentacles can "smell" its food in the water. Unchanged for millions of years, it is a formidable living fossil.

CEAN SUNFISH are occasional visitors to the reefs, traveling great distances to have their parasites removed by cleanerfish. They spend their lives in the open sea, swimming sluggishly near the surface and feeding on a diet of plankton and jellyfish. Weighing up to a ton, they can grow to ten feet in length, yet the spinal cord is only half an inch long, smaller than their rather modest brain. They swim slowly, moving their dorsal and anal fins sideways in a sculling motion, their tiny pectoral fins acting as stabilizers. They depend on their leathery skin and three-inch layer of gristle for protection. Too tough for harpooners, it has proved impervious even to rifle bullets. When shot, the Ocean Sunfish are said to make hideous groans by grinding their pharyngeal teeth, no doubt in rage. They are extremely vulnerable when small, but each female can release millions of eggs and the larvae, only an eighth of an inch long, are soon covered with long sharp spines, which deter many of their predators. From so many eggs enough will survive to carry on the species.

Octopus are not fish, nor are they even vertebrates, but they are smarter than most fishes in the sea. These most intelligent of all *cephalopods* can learn in captivity how to get shrimp out of a corked bottle just by watching another octopus do it. They swim by using jet propulsion, or scuttle over the reef, rapidly changing skin color and texture to match the background. The octopus will flush deeply when angered or frightened; while courting, a rainbow of colors passes over its body, pulsating in stripes and waves. If pursued it can eject a cloud of ink as a decoy while it escapes. Each of the eight arms, studded with sensitive suction discs, can reach under rocks and move them to get at its prey. An octopus often gathers crabs or mollusks to take back to its cave, where it opens them with its sharp beak, throwing the shells out the front door.

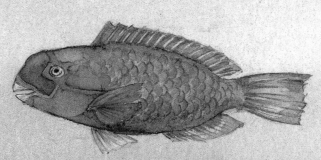

PARROTFISH, whose extravagant colors are as gaudy as those of any tropical bird, actually get their name from their teeth. A male **Sipadan Parrotfish** displays his large teeth, fused into a massive beak with which he chisels algae from the coral rock. All parrotfish ingest great quantities of coral, which they grind with a set of flat molarlike teeth in the throat. The rock and coral are crushed to a fine sand and the algae and coral polyps are absorbed. As they graze, each parrotfish excretes a small cloud of sand every few minutes, producing up to ten pounds a day. Groups of feeding parrotfish have been compared to herds of buffalo and, like grazers on land, can cause serious erosion. But these **Egghead Parrotfish** are also helping to create the many sandy beaches found near coral reefs.

After feeding up to ten hours a day, at night parrotfish fall into a deep sleep wedged in rock or coral caves. A **Palenose Parrotfish** secretes a mucous cocoon around himself to block his scent from night predators like moray eels, who hunt by smell. Many parrotfish return to the same shelter each night; some even find the way to their beds by orientation to the setting sun.

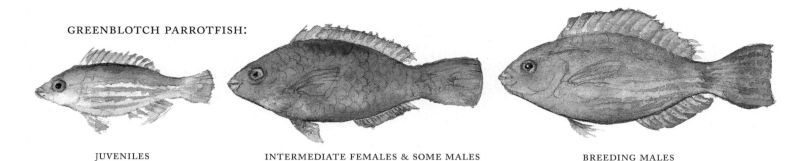

GREENBLOTCH PARROTFISH:

JUVENILES   INTERMEDIATE FEMALES & SOME MALES   BREEDING MALES

PARROTFISH begin as drab little fish and pass through a rainbow of colors as they grow. The dull colors of the juveniles hide them when they are most vulnerable; the colors of the intermediate females and the young males help them melt into the group to avoid predators. Parrotfish are "sequential hermaphrodites": they all start their lives as members of one sex but some of them change into the opposite sex. Many of the brilliantly colored breeding males were once females who changed sex. The brightest colors go to the dominant males, displaying their social status to intimidate the lesser males and to bedazzle the females. Thus many of the most favorable genes go into the great parrotfish gene pool.

Among the **Bicolor Parrotfish** of the Pacific, spawning occurs toward sunset and is often a group affair. After establishing territories in the current at the edge of the reef, the males begin to swim in circles, their mouths wide open, as a group of females hovers nearby. Sometimes the male is ignored by one female after another. Finally one allows him to come near and they swim side by side, faster and faster, rising as they move away from the reef. As they reach the surface they release eggs and sperm at the same time. The outgoing tide carries the fertilized eggs toward the relative safety of the open sea. Often the same current, turning in a gyre, will later bring the young fish *back* to the reef, where, like all juveniles, this bicolor keeps a low profile. His disruptive color pattern will actually help camouflage him on the reef.

QUEEN is a popular name often given to tropical reef fishes because of their beautiful colors. The glowing **Queen Triggerfish** (shown darkened as it is being groomed by a cleaner wrasse, and paler as it swims away) is extravagantly shaped and patterned, its fins and tail extended by long filaments, and its face and eyes adorned with brilliant blue lines—an exotic underwater makeup.

The **Queen Angelfish** is embellished with gold spots on its blue and yellow scales, and wears a bright blue crown. Its elegant, curving fins, brilliant colors, and ornament make it one of the most spectacular fishes on Caribbean reefs. Angelfish, like most reef fish, have extremely good eyesight. Their eyes have powerful muscles to provide quick, sharp focusing and are set forward on their snouts giving them good binocular vision and a wide visual field. A rich supply of cone cells ensures keen color perception. Angelfish have subtle and rapid control over the colors they display: by expanding and contracting color cells they can turn shades of glowing blue or yellow as they glide regally over the reef.

Many coral reef fish are sexually dimorphic, the male and female so unlike that they have often been thought to belong to two different species. Juveniles, who resemble neither parent, are even harder to identify for in many wrasse species they all look alike. The **Queen Coris** male is larger than the female, but not more spectacular. It is the smaller, more brilliantly colored and resplendent female who can rightfully be called the Red Queen.

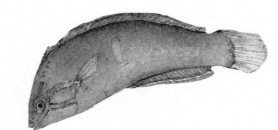

RAINBOW is another name inspired by the iridescent colors of many reef fishes, from Rainbow Fairy Basslets and Rainbow Parrotfish to Rainbow Scorpionfish. The **Rainbow Wrasse**, or **Yellow-tailed Coris** (above), is the same genus as the **Queen Coris**, or **Red-tailed Wrasse**, shown in Q, but a different species. Because scientists need to identify fishes precisely in order to exchange information, they always use the fishes' unique Latinized names, in this case *Coris gaimard* and *Coris frerei*.

Razorfish are daytime grazers of seagrass beds and sandy bottoms, feeding on the small invertebrates that live there in profusion. They have muted colors, for these are very dangerous places—the hunting grounds of many reef predators—and there are no coral caves or crevices to hide in. The **Green Razorfish** can escape by changing its color, bending its body to blend into the grass, or dive into the sand, where it keeps on swimming.

Masked Rabbitfish, named for their rabbity faces and voracious appetites, look like a pair of bandits as they prowl the sand flats. Unlike terrestrial rabbits, they carry deadly weapons—venomous spines in their dorsal and anal fins. But they are strict vegetarians, nibbling on seagrasses and algal fronds.

The **Bluespotted Sting Ray** lies motionless on the bottom, often hidden up to its turreted eyes in the sand. Breathing through spiracles, holes located behind the eyes, it preys on crabs, mollusks, and worms rooted out of the sand, grinding them up with its flat teeth. The sharp and venomous spine in its whiplike tail can inflict an extremely painful wound. All rays are fertilized internally and give birth to live young nourished within the uterus.

SQUIRRELFISH & SOLDIERFISH shun the daylight, hiding in the shadow of caves and ledges, which they defend with fierce territorial displays and sharp, chattering cries. Like cardinalfish, they hunt in the nighttime reefs, emerging only after the sun has set. As the light fades, their red color appears gray, then black, hiding them from larger predators, while their wide, saucerlike eyes allow them to see in almost total darkness. Some feed on the abundant night plankton, or on smaller fishes; others seek the myriad invertebrates that teem on the bottom at night.

Twilight is the time of greatest peril for the reef fishes. Daytime grazers seeking shelter in coral crevices become vulnerable as their sharp eyes falter in the dimming light. The night feeders peering cautiously from their sleeping places are also at risk, for their eyes need time to adjust to the darkness. As the shadows lengthen, the fishes gather in small groups close to the reef, milling about, hesitant and fearful. But they are hungry and must move out to prey on smaller fishes feeding on the swarms of plankton, and the crustaceans and mollusks that emerge at night. Caribbean **Schoolmasters** and **Mutton Snappers** begin to hunt the **Copper Sweepers**, tiny, iridescent fish that form tightly massed schools that forage in open water throughout the night.

Far above the small hunters and grazers the deadliest predators of the reef circle silently: the **Requiem Sharks**. With bodies shaped and senses honed by over three hundred million years of evolution, they are one of the oldest and most successful families in the sea. As the water darkens, they move in quickly, for their senses are far sharper in the half light than those of their prey. **Blacktip Sharks** stalk the hunting snappers, using all their senses: sight, smell, and sound—they even "hear" vibrations made in the water by swimming fish and the faint electric charge they produce at rest. Far below, a young **Reef Shark** skims the bottom in hot pursuit of a **Squirrelfish**.

IN THE DARKNESS of a Pacific night, more and more fishes come out to feed at the base of the coral reef. Young **Harlequin** and **Oriental Sweetlips** flutter like clowns, but their play is in deadly earnest. By mimicking the colors and movements of the gaudy, toxic **Sea Slugs**, like the **Spanish Dancer**, many can escape being eaten. As they grow they take on conservative stripes and spots and give up their cavorting to swim sedately, feeding on invertebrates through the night. **Snappers** are everywhere, eating worms, barnacles, mollusks, shrimps, crabs, and any fish they can catch. **Whitetip Sharks** are active all night, circling constantly, waiting to strike. Sinister **Scorpionfish** lurk motionless on the bottom, so well disguised they are virtually invisible—until what appears to be an algae-encrusted rock or bit of rubble suddenly opens great jaws, and a passing fish vanishes. Lolling about nearby and looking a bit foolish, a **Spotted Soapfish** seems harmless, but is far from it. Protected by a toxic mucous that deters almost all predators, it roams freely over the reef, devouring countless crustaceans and fishes almost as large as itself. On the bottom, a **Starry Moray Eel** hunts crabs, snails, shrimps, and other crustaceans in total darkness, guided only by its phenomenal sense of smell.

EVEN BEFORE SUNRISE nocturnal fishes turn toward the safety of the reef, and as the sea slowly brightens, daytime browsers begin to emerge. Among the late risers are **Bluelined Surgeonfish**, algal farmers who must defend their plots against nomadic grazers, like the **Orangeband Surgeonfish**. Surgeons are well armed; with hinged scalpels set in grooves at the base of the caudal fin, a quick flick of the tail will inflict a painful wound. **Shrimpfish**, or Razorfish, also carry knives for their scales are fused into a razor-sharp edge along the belly. But these slender fish would rather hide than fight. Hanging head down among red and white sea whips, they pluck tiny invertebrates from the water with their tubelike mouths.

TANG is another name for certain Surgeonfish, and refers to the sharp scalpels they carry for intimidation and defense in their frequent territorial disputes. These weapons, often outlined in highly visible colors, serve as warnings: a blue **Regal** or **Palette Tang** sports a yellow triangle around its hidden knife; the scabbard of the **Achilles Tang** is a brilliant orange against its black body; and the **Whitecheek Tang** wears a pattern of bright stripes pointing toward its yellow sheath. Like all surgeons, tangs go through many color changes to warn or threaten other fishes, frequently other tangs, who are often their worst enemies.

Schools of **Convict Tangs** are nomadic, browsing on algae wherever they find it, which is often on the territory of a smaller, algal-farming **Lavender Tang**. The angry farmer rushes out to defend his plot, a dark outline visible around his head and body. The Convict Tangs respond by "mobbing" him: forming lines of up to a hundred fish, they descend one at a time to feed. As the Lavender slams into the Convict, the feeding fish seems to flee but instead rises up and moves off to graze farther along. Another descends, eats a bit, and in turn is driven off, only to continue feeding in another spot as the next engages the farmer. If the farmers do not band together, such tactics soon overwhelm the lone Lavender's defenses.

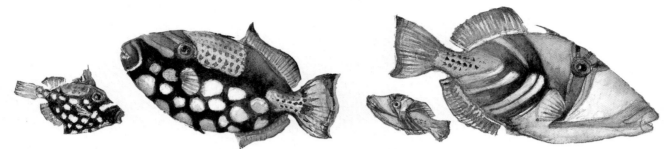

TRIGGERFISH have deep, flattened bodies, providing a broad surface for the spectacular patterns of the **Clown** and **Picasso Triggerfish,** shown above with their juveniles. Conspicuous in open water or in an aquarium, these patterns form a baffling target to predators as the triggerfish thread their way through the maze of coral. They feed on invertebrates, and their strong, chisel-like teeth can bite through the shells of most crustaceans. The **Blue & Gold Triggerfish** even overcomes the formidable defenses of the black sea urchin by blowing a jet of water from its mouth, turning the urchin over to feast on the soft underbelly. Its eyes, set far back on its long head, are safely out of reach of the urchin's sharp, venomous spines.

Triggerfish also have ingenious spines: their long first dorsal spine can be raised and locked in position by a second one, the "trigger." At a sign of danger, or when bedding down for the night, a triggerfish will wedge itself into a crevice and erect the spine. Some triggerfish also protect their vulnerable eggs. The female undulates her fins to hollow out a nest in the sand, and lays a cluster of eggs, often weighing down the buoyant eggs with bits of rubble. One or both parents then guard them from hungry egg thieves.

The **Trumpetfish** is a sneaky fish, changeable as a chameleon. He can assume many colors and patterns as he swims leisurely through the reef, hovering at an angle to hide among the slender seagrasses and sea fans. He hunts other fishes by stealth, often changing only the color of his head so that he seems to be just another small, innocent browser. But his best trick, called "shadow-stalking," is to swim alongside a fish that eats only plants or invertebrates, using it as a cover. Loitering on the back of a **Goldmann's Sweetlips,** who eats only crabs and mollusks, this one easily mimics the color and sometimes the spots of its dorsal fin and tail.

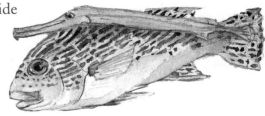

NICORNFISH are surgeonfish named for the hornlike projections that sprout from their foreheads as they mature. They migrate in large schools to the outer reef edges, where they feed on the abundant brown algae and plankton brought in by the offshore currents. The **Bluespine Unicornfish,** feeding above in the letter U, is drab in color, but its sharp spines, which discourage its many predators, are outlined in bright blue. Its short, stout horn is an imposing deterrent as well. But many unicorns have no horns at all. **Vlaming's Unicornfish** develop instead a large bump on the snout, often an intense blue or yellow, and trail long, delicate filaments from each lobe of the tail. When in prime breeding condition their markings turn an iridescent blue in spectacular courting displays, which show off their male fitness and desirability, and entice the females to spawn. The handsome **Spotted Unicornfish** (left) bears the characteristic strong tapering horn, which serves him against other males in territorial disputes and whose splendor impresses his females.

Another hornless species, the **Orangespine Unicornfish,** gathers in shoals at the edges of the reef to spawn during the new and full moon, when the tide is at its peak. Although this is the most dangerous time for the adults, it is the safest for their young, for the ebb tide will carry the fertilized eggs far out into the relative safety of the open ocean. The adults are at risk but their larvae have a better chance to survive.

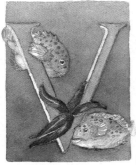

VELVETFISH are tiny oval fish whose skin is covered with fleshy bumps that give it a knobby, velvety texture. They spend their entire lives within certain corals, hiding between branches, a habit that has earned them another name: Coral Crouchers. They have very small pelvic fins, which they hardly need, for Velvetfish rarely swim more than a few inches from their coral homes. Feeding on shrimp and plankton brought by the current, these fish use their fins to wedge themselves into the coral. So tight is the fit that when coral is brought to the surface and the fish tumble out they come as a great surprise. Only a few species are known, among them the **Spotted Velvetfish,** in the letter V, the **Madagascar Velvetfish,** shown lifesize, and the one-inch **Pygmy Coral Croucher,** emerging briefly from its coral castle.

The red **Velvet Sea Star** seems harmless, but sea stars are relentless predators, creeping about on their many tube feet to pry open clams, scallops, and other mollusks with their powerful suckers. As the shellfish tires it opens slightly and the sea star turns its stomach inside out, inserting it into the narrow gap, where it digests the helpless victim inside its own shell. To escape its own predators a sea star can sever an arm from its body and scuttle away on the remaining four. Not only does the arm grow back, but another sea star will regenerate from the abandoned arm, for its internal organs are replicated in each segment of its body. This **Blue Sea Star,** like all sea stars, can perform these amazing feats with no detectable brain.

The **Crown-of-Thorns Starfish** is a walking fortress of venomous spines that threatens the very body of the reef. Engulfing live coral in a spiny embrace, these grisly sea stars evert their stomachs to digest the coral polyps *inside* their stony skeletons. Virtually impregnable, they can quickly decimate a reef, for each devours two square feet of coral a day. But two tiny crustaceans that live in the coral, a pistol shrimp and a trapezia crab, rush out to protect their home. By snapping at the sea star's arms and gnawing its tube feet, they may even succeed in driving it away.

WRASSES OF THE GREAT BARRIER REEF

SOUTHERN TUBELIP

BLACK-SPOTTED WRASSE, INITIAL & TERMINAL PHASES

DIANA'S HOGFISH

LYRETAIL HOGFISH

CHISELTOOTH WRASSE

GOLDSTRIPE WRASSE

VIOLET-LINED MAORI WRASSE RED PHASE

BI-COLOR CLEANER WRASSE

REDBREASTED MAORI WRASSE

BREASTSPOT CLEANER WRASSE

VIOLET-LINED MAORI WRASSE STREAKED PHASE

DUSKY WRASSE

SPOTTED WRASSE

FEMININE WRASSE

OCELLATED WRASSE

WRASSES are among the most beautiful fishes on the reef and also some of the most fascinating to watch. Unlike many fishes who hang out in schools of look-alikes, wrasses are flashy individualists, with intricate patterns and brilliant colors. Their sex lives are colorful, too, for cross-dressing and sex change are the rule, not the exception. Many wrasses, like the sleek blue **Sunset Wrasse** and the **Peacock Wrasse** (here in spectacular courting display), are solitary, secretive fish, often seen swimming about, sculling with their pectoral fins, their tails hanging languidly behind them. Voracious eaters—their family name, Labridae, means "greedy"—wrasses are the first to appear at any feeding opportunity, gorging on clams, crabs, and other crustaceans stirred up by larger fishes and by human divers.

Other wrasses are hardworking entrepreneurs, the cleaning professionals who provide fishes with essential grooming services that free them from dangerous parasites. These small wrasses set up a cleaning stations near a prominent landmark, like the letter W above, where the fishes wait in line. A **Moon Wrasse** and a long-nosed **Bird Wrasse** hang suspended nearby while a **Checkerboard Wrasse,** whose double set of sharp teeth can make short work of any small fish, is tended by a **Bi-color Cleaner Wrasse,** whom it scrupulously refrains from biting.

Wrasses are timid fish and become uneasy in dimming light. The **Clown Coris,** the female shown here with a juvenile (often called the **Twin-spot Wrasse**), will dive into the sand when the sky clouds over, lying on its side just under the surface. As evening approaches the wrasses are the first to retire, some spinning mucous cocoons as they settle on the bottom, others wedging themselves between rocks or burrowing into the sand. They are deep sleepers and the last fish to arise in the morning. It has been reported that some wrasses sleeping in a Bermuda aquarium were found to fall into REM sleep, the state that in higher vertebrates is often associated with dreaming.

WRASSES abound on Indo-Pacific reefs, with more species than any family except that of the ubiquitous gobies. But counting them is not easy: the tiny gobies hide most of the day, and wrasses disappear for twelve hours every night. Identification is even more problematic, for wrasses are the most changeable of fishes. The **Chameleon Wrasse** (above), from the Galapagos, is a typical wrasse: constantly on the move, zigzagging about the reef, rapidly changing colors and pattern. An individual male, normally blue with an orange head, can suddenly darken, turn red like a female, or fade to white as it passes from coral heads to the sandy bottom; its stripes and spots can appear and disappear as it emerges from deep shadows under ledges to the sunlit open water.

Even more complex changes occur as they grow. Atlantic **Bluehead Wrasse** juveniles are white or yellow, sometimes with a black stripe. Initially, all adults are yellow with a dark stripe and white bars; males and females look alike and spawn in groups, usually at midday. A few adults become supermales with green bodies and iridescent blue heads; some of these are former high-ranking *females,* who changed color and sex to become males. The supermales are larger and more powerful swimmers and each dominates a harem of females while bullying the lesser males to keep them from mating. Occasionally some of these manage to "streak spawn": by passing as females they sneak in on a spawning pair to add their sperm—and their genes—to the next generation.

If supermales are sometimes fooled, ichthyologists, the scientists who study fishes, are often baffled. Some color forms and many male and female patterns—like those of the Pacific **Three-lined Wrasse**—are so different they were thought to be separate species. It is no wonder that wrasse taxonomy is in a state of constant flux, as more wrasses are found to be color differences within a species.

EVOLUTION has provided the wrasses with amazing teeth: one or more pairs of protruding canines plus a set of grinding molars in their throats. The blue canines of the **Harlequin Tuskfish** protrude and interlock, enabling it to comb through rubble and seize any crustaceans it exposes. The **Dragon Wrasse** is often called the **Rockmover Wrasse** for its zeal in turning over rocks with its teeth, as it searches for bottom-dwelling invertebrates. Anything is grist to its pharyngeal mill: gastropods, bivalves, sea urchins, brittle stars, and crabs. Its tasseled juvenile resembles an algal fragment, and survives by mimicking its movements. At almost the same size, the beautifully colored **Exquisite Wrasse** is already an adult, with tiny teeth and its own bifocals: its corneas are divided, providing close-up lenses that can focus on the microscopic floating plankton on which it feeds.

The **Slingjaw Wrasse,** who hunts by stealth, has evolved a devastatingly effective mouth. Part of its jaw, folded under the chin, can be shot forward half the length of its body to envelop swimming shrimps and fishes, or snatch crabs and mollusks from their hiding places in the coral.

Wrasses are cleaners as juveniles, and some continue to do so as adults. They use their specialized teeth like tweezers to remove parasites and dead tissue from fishes, large and small. Even the six-foot **Napoleon Wrasse** will go into a passive trance while being cleaned, letting them swim about in its massive mouth and gills. Their striped pattern and sinuous dance identify them as cleaners, and protect them from being eaten.

55

DRAWN TO SCALE THE NAPOLEON WRASSE WOULD BE
TWICE THE SIZE OF THIS PAGE.

iphasia setifer is the scientific name for the **Hair-tailed Blenny,** one of the fang blennies, named for its long, curving canine teeth and hairy tail. This name, which means "swordlike" and "bristle-bearing," is one of those long, tongue-twisting Latinized names that we find so intimidating from the mouths of ichthyologists (the "fish discoursers" or "those who talk about fish"). These names are the only ones used by scientists, for they provide exact identification of any fish, enabling scientists to share precise information with others, in any language, anywhere in the world.

A fish can have many common names, often colorful but usually confusing. One family called Serranids (from the Latin *serra* or "saw") includes Coral Trout, Rock Cod, Potato, Tomato, and Strawberry Cod, even a Trout Cod! Others, like those swimming above, have been called Butterfly Perch, Lyre-tail Coralfish, Fairy Basslets, and recently **Redfin Anthias.** But to the ichthyologist these fish are *Pseudanthias dispar.* The Latin name, always italicized, is in two parts: the first word is capitalized and refers to the *genus* (plural *genera*), a grouping of closely related fishes in a family; the second is lowercase and names the *species,* the basic unit of a population whose members breed successfully with one another. They represent the natural, fundamental building blocks of bio-diversity, essential elements in the study of what Darwin called the "mystery of mysteries": the origin of species.

Consider the tiny **Flashlightfish,** who swim about in the dark, glowing like fireflies. Their scientific name, *Photoblepharon palpebratus,* means "light-eyelid" and "blinking." Each fish carries a light, created by luminous bacteria that live in sacs below each eye. He blinks them off and on to lure his prey, to signal other fish, and to confuse his predators. It is a vivid, accurate name, and is also part of a much larger system of classification that indicates not only how he is related to other fish, but to all other creatures, including ourselves. Called taxonomy (from a Greek word that means "to put in order"), this system, devised by Linnaeus in the eighteenth century, is still used to comprehend the profusion, diversity, and evolution of life on earth—and in the coral seas.

ELLOW is the most common color on reef fishes, and the most visible, especially on sunlit coral heads. Colors of various wavelengths are rapidly absorbed by seawater: red disappears first, then orange, blue, and green, but yellow can still be distinguished at 300 feet. The **Golden Damselfish**, a territorial algae feeder on deepwater corals, is an intense chrome yellow. Its high visibility ensures that the damsel's vigorous defense of his territory is seen by other damsels, protecting his algal plot and hidden nest of eggs.

Almost all coral-grazing butterflyfish are brightly patterned and most have yellow somewhere on their bodies. The **Yellowhead Butterflyfish** in the letter Y has a conspicuous and distinctive color pattern, unique to her species and instantly recognizable by her mate, from whom she is rarely parted. She wears her colors boldly, for she can see most daytime predators before they see her, and dart into the coral. The timid **Lemon Coral Gobies** lead hidden, solitary lives crouched in heads of branching coral, where their subtle colors conceal them from approaching predators. Yet at close range their colors help identify potential mates, while their blue lines warn others of their poisonous mucous. **Nudibranchs**, commonly called Sea Slugs, are snails without shells, soft mollusks whose vivid neon colors advertise their nasty taste and toxic secretions.

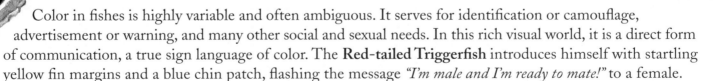

Color in fishes is highly variable and often ambiguous. It serves for identification or camouflage, advertisement or warning, and many other social and sexual needs. In this rich visual world, it is a direct form of communication, a true sign language of color. The **Red-tailed Triggerfish** introduces himself with startling yellow fin margins and a blue chin patch, flashing the message *"I'm male and I'm ready to mate!"* to a female. She responds by changing her body color, but only on the side facing him, to signal that she is willing, or that she is not interested. But the greatest color virtuosos of all are the boneless *cephalopods*: the octopus, the cuttlefish, and the **Caribbean Reef Squid,** who can instantly create intense waves of shimmering colors over its whole body.

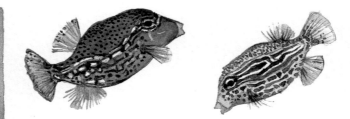

FLOATING BOXCARS, the Trunkfish, Boxfish, and Cowfish all belong to a curious group called "fish-with-shells" or "fish-in-a-box." Enclosed from head to tail in a bony covering of interlocking plates, they are understandably poor swimmers. Fluttering their fins and sculling with their tails, they bumble along the bottom in short spurts, biting off bits of coral with beaklike teeth to nibble on coral polyps and snap up invertebrates. Nosing about in the ampersand above, the **Bluetail Trunkfish** and yellow **Cube Boxfish** can ignore most predators, protected by their sharp, bony armor and by a powerful toxin they can release at will. Both male and female **Scribbled Boxfish** are elaborately patterned, the male in brilliant blues, the female in startling yellow and black. These bold colors serve as highly visible underwater warning labels to predators: "*This package contains a deadly poison.*"

The **Longhorn Cowfish,** with horns on both ends of his body, is easily recognizable in this mug shot. A well-known grazer on the seagrass flats of the Great Barrier Reef, he may not be able to change his rigid bony shape, but he can change his spots from blue to brown, his skin from tan to orange, or fade away to white when swimming over the sandy bottom.

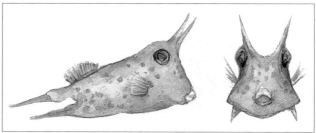

Another fiercely armored fish, its body encased in hard, bony plates studded with spines, is the **Knightfish** or **Pineconefish** of Australia. Banding together at night, they hunt down small invertebrates in caves and under ledges, aided by light from colonies of luminous bacteria living in pockets in their jaws. This symbiotic alliance is only one of many that allow the reef creatures to use every possible niche in their crowded habitat.

SEAHORSES & PIPEFISHES are true bony fishes, but like the Boxfish they also wear bones on the outside: their segmented bodies are encased in rings of armor derived from modified scales. Their family name, Sygnathidae, refers to the long tubular snouts with which they siphon tiny crustaceans from the water. Pipefishes, which look like stretched-out seahorses, swim either horizontally or vertically, but the Seahorse or *Hippocampus* (horse-caterpillar) swims upright. Propelled only by the rapid motion of its tiny dorsal fin, it steers with its head and holds on to anything it can grasp with its prehensile tail. Seahorses are nearly invisible on the reef, for they match their color to their moorings—from red coral to purple sea fans and green or yellow seagrass, or, like the **Thorny Seahorse** (opposite) to a green ampersand.

Seahorses are famous for the role of the fathers: many male fishes guard and tend the eggs, but only the male seahorse becomes pregnant, fertilizing and incubating the eggs inside his body. **White's Seahorses** (above) are mating, but it is the male who receives the eggs in a special brood pouch. His pregnancy lasts three weeks, and the female visits him every day, ignoring all others. Entwining tails and vibrating their dorsal fins, they dance around his blade of grass. This ritual must strengthen their bond, for as soon as he delivers his brood, pumping them out in a long and arduous labor, he presents his empty pouch to his mate and she deposits more eggs.

The brilliantly striped **Banded Pipefish** male is also pregnant, but he carries the fragile eggs in a transparent sac suspended *under* his belly. Far less conservative, **Ornate Ghost Pipefish** dress like carnival dancers at Mardi Gras. They can change their colors in seconds, vanishing into the brilliant soft corals and eel grass beds. In this species it is the female who has a special open pouch between her pelvic fins and her body to brood and hatch the eggs.

PUFFERS swim about the reef with impunity, for these fish have a secret weapon. Any predator that tries to grab one is in for a big surprise: the little puffer instantly turns into a large, prickly ball that is difficult to bite, much less to swallow. The astonished predator spits it out and the puffer nonchalantly swims away. If his attacker tries again the puffer reinflates, rising to the surface to float, still impregnable, upside down. How does he do it? A ten-inch **Whitespotted Puffer** can pump a quart of water into a sac in his abdomen in seconds; out of the water he inflates with air, making an "uk-uk-uk" sound as he does.

Many of the most beautiful puffers, like the tiny **Spotted Sharpnose Puffer,** and ominous ones, like the **Masked Puffer,** have a second, terrible line of defense. Puffers carry one of the most deadly poisons in nature—tetrodotoxin— a potent neurotoxin that causes convulsions, paralysis, and a painful death. If very carefully prepared, puffers can be eaten safely, and in Japan many risk their lives just to taste the delectable puffer called *fugu*.

Porcupinefish are puffers with spikes. Their bodies are covered with long, stout, very sharp spines that lie flat against the skin until the fish inflates itself and the spines automatically erect, creating a round, hard ball bristling with daggers. Early Polynesians made war helmets out of the dried skins, and used a poison from the puffers to tip their arrows. Barracudas and sharks have the temerity to swallow both of these spiky fishes, but at no little risk, for sharks have been known to choke to death on a puffer stuck in its throat. What happens when a porcupinefish reaches its stomach, only the shark knows.

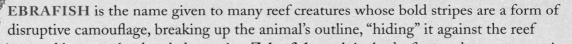

ZEBRAFISH is the name given to many reef creatures whose bold stripes are a form of disruptive camouflage, breaking up the animal's outline, "hiding" it against the reef background. The stripes and bars on the dreaded scorpion **Zebrafish** mask its body, fins, and venomous spines, enabling it to sneak up on dazzled fishes. A young **Zebra Moray's** contrasting bars shimmer as it stalks a **Zebra Crab** crouched on a sea urchin, the crab hidden by stripes that mimic those on the urchin's spines. As he browses on plankton, a **Zebra Angelfish** can afford to be conspicuous for he can quickly slip into a crevice when alarmed. His dark bars are a sign that he has reversed sex and is now a male with rights to a territory and to smaller, plainer females. The tremulous **Zebra Blenny** is always busy, dashing out to feed, then bolting back into her hole. Tenaciously territorial as well as skittish, her pattern helps her show off *and* hide out.

Zooxanthellae deserve the last word, for they are fundamental links in the complex web of coral reef life. These single-celled, yellow-brown algae live symbiotically within the tissues of the coral reef architects: the **Coral polyps**. Long thought to be plants, these polyps are tiny multicellular animals that form colonies numbering hundreds of thousands of individuals. Reefs are built from their linked stony skeletons that the polyps make from calcium in the seawater around them—but not by themselves. The zooxanthellae enable polyps to produce calcium carbonate up to ten times faster than they could alone. As plants, the algae depend on sunlight for photosynthesis, so reef-building corals flourish only as far down as the light penetrates, 100 to 150 feet. Over countless millennia, as the sea floor subsides and ancient reefs die, corals build on the skeletons of their ancestors, which go down much, much farther. Geologists drilling to reach the basaltic rock of the sea floor from a Pacific atoll found coral limestone at depths of more than a mile! Without the zooxanthellae, coral reefs could never keep pace with natural erosion and the gradual sinking of the ocean floor, but would slip beneath the sea and be lost in the darkness.

ZOOXANTHELLAE IN A CORAL POLYP

MAP OF THE CORAL REEFS

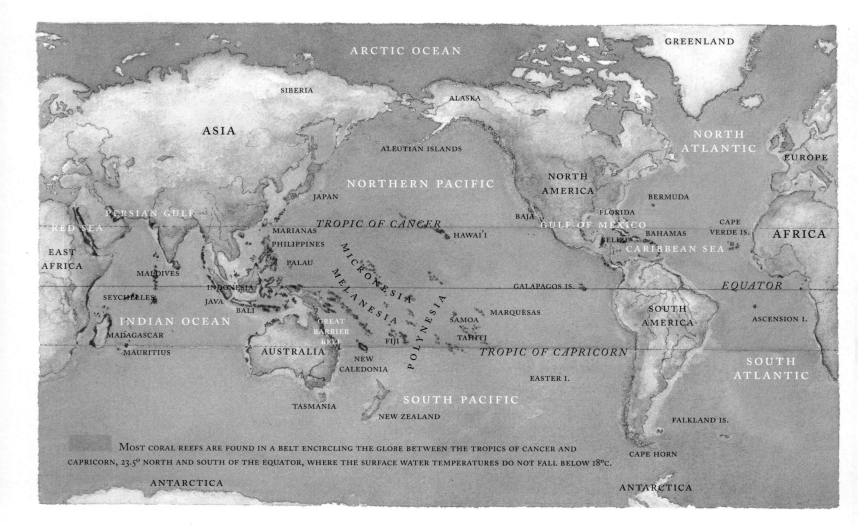

MOST CORAL REEFS ARE FOUND IN A BELT ENCIRCLING THE GLOBE BETWEEN THE TROPICS OF CANCER AND
CAPRICORN, 23.5° NORTH AND SOUTH OF THE EQUATOR, WHERE THE SURFACE WATER TEMPERATURES DO NOT FALL BELOW 18°C.

THE NAMES OF THE FISHES

(**Bold** type indicates fishes pictured in initial letters)

PAGE	COMMON NAME	SCIENTIFIC NAME	SIZE	RANGE
A 10	ATLANTIC ANGELFISHES:			
	Blue Angelfish & juvenile	*Holacanthus bermudensis*	18" (45.7 cm)	S. Florida, Bermuda, Bahamas
	Gray Angelfish	*Pomacanthus arcuatus*	14" (35.6 cm)	Atlantic coast, New England to Brazil
	French Angelfish & juvenile	*Pomacanthus paru*	13½" (34.3 cm)	Atlantic coast, New England to Brazil
	Rock Beauty & juv., int.	*Holacanthus tricolor*	12" (30.5 cm)	Bermuda, Bahamas, Florida, Caribbean
	Resplendent Pygmy Angelfish	*Centropyge resplendens*	2⅜" (6 cm)	Ascension Island (mid-Atlantic)
11	PACIFIC ANGELFISHES:			
	Emperor Angelfish	*Pomacanthus imperator*	**12" (30.5 cm)**	**Indo-Pacific**
	Yellowmask Angelfish	*Pomacanthus xanthometapon*	12⅝" (32 cm)	Indo-Pacific
	Emperor Angelfish & juvenile	*Pomacanthus imperator*	12" (30 cm)	Indo-Pacific
	Japanese Pygmy Angelfish	*Centropyge interrupta*	6" (15 cm)	Pacific Coast of Japan
12	**Scalefin Anthias**	*Pseudanthias squamipinnis*	**4½" (11 cm)**	**Indo-Pacific, Red Sea**
B 13	**Candy Basslet**	*Liopropoma sp.*	**2" (5 cm)**	**Caribbean, Bahamas**
	Royal Gramma	*Gramma loreto*	3" (8 cm)	Caribbean, Bahamas, Bermuda
	Blackcap Gramma	*Gramma melacara*	4" (10.2 cm)	Bahamas, Caribbean
	Narrow-banded Batfish	*Platax orbicularis*	20" (50 cm)	Indo-central Pacific
	Barracuda	*Sphyraena barracuda*	72" (183 cm)	Tropical Seas
14	**Ringed Blenny**	*Starksia hassi*	**1½" (4 cm)**	**Bahamas, Caribbean**
	Diamond Blenny	*Malacoctenus boehlkei*	**2½" (6.4 cm)**	**Bahamas, Caribbean**
	Longhorn Blenny	*Hypsoblennius exstochilus*	2" (5 cm)	Bahamas
	Downy Blenny	*Labrisomus kalisherae*	3" (7.5 cm)	W. Atlantic, Florida, Brazil
	Secretary Blenny	*Acanthemblemaria maria*	2" (5 cm)	Bahamas, Caribbean
	Bluelined Sabretooth Blenny	*Plagiotremus rhinorhyncos*	4¾" (12 cm)	Indo-central Pacific, S.E. Asia

15	**White-face Butterflyfish**	*Chaetodon mesoleucos*	6⅜" (16 cm)	**Red Sea**
	Fourspot Butterflyfish	*Chaetodon quadrimaculatus*	6⅜" (16 cm)	Pacific Ocean
	Crown Butterflyfish	*Chaetodon paucifasciatus*	5½" (14 cm)	Red Sea, Gulf of Aden
	Triangular Butterflyfish	*Chaetodon triangulum*	6" (15 cm)	Indian Ocean, W. Indonesia

C

16	**Flamefish Cardinal**	*Apogon maculatus*	4" (10.2 cm)	W. Atlantic
	Yellow-lined Cardinalfish	*Apogon cyanosoma*	3¼" (8 cm)	Indonesia, Australia
	Eight-lined Cardinalfish	*Cheilodipterus sp.*	8½" (22 cm)	Indonesia, Australia
	Pajama Cardinalfish	*Sphaeramia nematoptera*	3¼" (8 cm)	Indonesia, Australia
	Conchfish	*Astrapogon stellatus*	2¾" (7 cm)	W. Atlantic, Florida, Caribbean
	Queen Conchfish	*Strombus gigas* Linnaeus	12" (30 cm)	S. Florida, Bahamas, Caribbean
17	Cubbyu	*Pareques umbrosus*	10" (25.4 cm)	Florida to N. Carolina, Gulf of Mexico
	Cleaner Shrimp	*Lysmata amboinensis*	1½" (4 cm)	Florida, Bahamas, Caribbean
	Cube (or Yellow) Boxfish	*Ostracion cubicus*	18" (45.7 cm)	Indo-west Pacific
	Cleaning Goby	*Gobiosoma genie*	1½" (4 cm)	Bahamas, Cayman Islands
	Coney	*Cephalopholis fulvus*	10" (25.4 cm)	Caribbean, Florida to Brazil
	Boxer Crab	*Lybia tessellata*	¾" (2 cm)	Indo-west Pacific, Indonesia

D

18	**Ambon Damselfish, blue and yellow forms**	*Pomacentrus amboinensis*	4¼" (11 cm)	**Indo-west Pacific**
	Blue-green Chromis	*Chromis viridis*	3½" (9 cm)	Indo-west Pacific
	Clown Anemonefish	*Amphiprion percula*	2⅜" (6 cm)	Indo-west Pacific, Australia
19	Spiny Chromis	*Acanthochromis polyacanthus*	5⅞" (15 cm)	Indo-Australian Archipelago
	Three-spot Damselfish	*Stegastes planifrons*	3½" (9 cm)	W. Atlantic, Caribbean
	Blue-green Chromis (night color)	*Chromis viridis*	3½" (9 cm)	Indo-west Pacific

E

20	**Banded Moray Eel**	*Gymnothorax rueppelliae*	32" (81.3 cm)	**Indo-Pacific, Hawai'i**
	Dwarf Moray	*Gymnothorax melatremus*	10¼" (26 cm)	**Indo-Pacific, Hawai'i**
	Chain Moray	*Echidna catenata*	28" (71 cm)	W. Atlantic, Bahamas
	Blue-ribbon Eel	*Rhinomuraena quaesita*	32" (81.3 cm)	Indo-Pacific
	Goldentail Moray	*Gymnothorax miliaris*	24" (61 cm)	W. Atlantic
	Spotted Garden Eel	*Heteroconger hassi*	24" (61 cm)	Indo-Pacific, Red Sea
	Spotted Snake Eel	*Myrichthys maculosus*	20" (50.8 cm)	Indo-Pacific, Red Sea

#	Common Name	Scientific Name	Size	Range
21	**Spangled Emperor**	*Lethrinus nebulosus*	34½" (87.6 cm)	**Indo-Pacific, Red Sea, Australia**
	Bigeye Emperor	*Monotaxis grandoculus*	24" (61 cm)	Indo-Pacific
	Trumpet Emperor	*Lethrinus miniatus*	36" (91.4 cm)	W. Pacific
	Golden-lined Emperor	*Gnathodentex aurolineatus*	10" (25 cm)	Indo-Pacific
22	**Goldband (or Van Gogh) Fusilier**	*Pterocaesio chrysozona*	7" (18 cm)	**Indo-Pacific**
	Longnose Filefish	*Oxymonacanthus longirostris*	3½" (9 cm)	Indo-Pacific, Australia
	Mimic Filefish	*Paraluteres prionurus*	4" (10 cm)	Indo-Pacific, Australia
	Saddleback Puffer	*Canthigaster valentini*	4" (10 cm)	Indo-Pacific, Hawai'i, Australia
	Wirenet Filefish	*Cantherinus pardalis*	10" (25 cm)	Indo-Pacific, Red Sea
23	Panther Flounder	*Bothus pantherinus*	12" (30 cm)	Indo-Pacific, Red Sea, Hawai'i
	Peacock Flounder	*Bothus lunatus*	18" (45.7 cm)	E. Atlantic, Bermuda to Brazil
	Giant Frogfish	*Antennarius commersonii*	10⅝" (27 cm)	Indo-Pacific, Red Sea, Hawai'i
24	**Dash & Dot Goatfish**	*Parupeneus barberinus*	16" (40.6 cm)	**Indo-west Pacific**
	Maiden Goby	*Valenciennea puellaris*	5½" (14 cm)	**Indo-west Pacific**
	Red Sea Bird Wrasse	*Gomphosus caeruleus*	12" (30 cm)	Red Sea, Arabian Sea
	Red Sea (or Forsskal's) Goatfish	*Parupeneus forsskali*	11" (28 cm)	Red Sea, Gulf of Aden
	French Grunt	*Haemulon flavolineatum*	12" (30 cm)	W. Atlantic, S. Carolina to Brazil
	Porkfish	*Anisotremus virginicus*	16" (40.6 cm)	W. Atlantic, Florida to Brazil
25	**Rusty Goby**	*Priolepis hipoliti*	1" (2.5 cm)	**Florida, Bahamas, Caribbean**
	Greenbanded Goby	*Gobiosoma multifasciatum*	1¾" (4.4 cm)	**Bahamas, Caribbean**
	Galapagos Blue-banded Goby	*Lythrypnus gilberti*	1¼" (3.2 cm)	**Galapagos Islands**
	Maori Goby	*Gobiodon histrio*	2⅜" (6 cm)	West & Central Pacific
	Wheeler's Shrimp Goby	*Amblyeleotris wheeleri*	2⅝" (6.7 cm)	Indo-west Pacific
	Alpheid Shrimp	*Alpheus ochrostriatus*	2" (5 cm)	Red Sea to Indonesia, Fiji to Japan
	Signal Goby	*Signigobius biocellatus*	2⅝" (6.7 cm)	Indo-Australian Archipelago
26	VARIATIONS IN INDO-PACIFIC GROUPERS:			
	Red-spotted Rock Cod	*Cephalopholis leopardus*	8" (20 cm)	Indo-central Pacific
	Coronation Trout	*Variola louti*	20" (50.8 cm)	Indo-west Pacific
	Honeycomb Cod	*Epinephelus merra* Bloch	11" (28 cm)	Indo-central Pacific
	Coral Trout	*Plectropomus leopardus*	28" (71 cm)	W. Pacific
	Polka Dot Coral Trout	*Plectropomus areolatus*	28" (71 cm)	Indo-west Pacific
	Potato Cod	*Epinephelus tukula*	56" (142.2 cm)	Indo-west Pacific

	Highfin Coral Trout	*Plectropomus oligocanthus*	26" (66 cm)	W. Pacific
	Camouflage Grouper	*Epinephelus polyphekadion*	24" (61 cm)	Indo-central Pacific
	Peacock Grouper	*Cephalopholis argus*	20" (50.8 cm)	Indo-central Pacific
	Six-banded Rock Cod	*Cephalopholis sexmaculata*	18¾" (47.6 cm)	Indo-central Pacific
	Barramundi Cod	*Cromileptes altivelis*	16" (40.6 cm)	W. Pacific
27	**Coral Grouper**	***Cephalopholis miniata***	**16" (40.6 cm)**	**Indo-west Pacific**
	Nassau Grouper	*Epinephelus striatus*	36" (91 cm)	N. Carolina, Bermuda to Brazil
	Tiger Grouper	*Mycteroperca tigris*	36" (91 cm)	S. Florida, Bermuda to Brazil
28	**Freckled Hawkfish**	***Paracirrhites forsteri***	**8" (20 cm)**	**Indo-central Pacific, Indo-Australia**
	Humbug	***Dascyllus melanurus***	**2¾" (7 cm)**	**W. Pacific, Australia**
	Tartan (or Longnose) Hawkfish	*Oxycirrhitus typus*	4" (10 cm)	Indo-Pacific
	Pixy Hawkfish	*Cirrhitichthys oxycephalus*	2⅜" (6 cm)	Indo-Pacific
	Butter Hamlet	*Hypoplectrus unicolor*	5¼" (13 cm)	Bermuda, Florida, Bahamas
	Golden Hamlet	*Hypoplectrus gummigutta*	5¼" (13 cm)	S. Florida, West Indies
	Shy Hamlet	*Hypoplectrus guttavarius*	5¼" (13 cm)	Florida Keys to West Indies
	Barred Hamlet	*Hypoplectrus puella*	5¼" (13 cm)	Florida, Bermuda to West Indies
29	Halfbeak	*Hemiramphus balao*	14" (35.6 cm)	East & West Atlantic
	Houndfish	*Tylosurus crocodilus*	52" (132 cm)	Circumtropical
	Dwarf Herring	*Jenkinsia lamprotaenia*	2½" (6.4 cm)	Florida, Bahamas, Caribbean
	Blue Hamlet	*Hypoplectrus gemma*	5¼" (13 cm)	S. Florida, Florida Keys
	Indigo Hamlet	*Hypoplectrus indigo*	5¼" (13 cm)	S. Florida, Bahamas
	Yellowtail Hamlet	*Hypoplectrus chlorurus*	5¼" (13 cm)	West Indies, Venezuela
	Black Hamlet	*Hypoplectrus nigricans*	5¼" (13 cm)	Florida to Bahamas, West Indies
30	**Idol of the Moors (Moorish Idol)**	***Zanclus cornutus***	**9½" (24 cm)**	**Indo-Pacific to Mexico**
	Pennant Bannerfish	*Heniochus chrystostomus*	7" (18 cm)	West & Central Pacific
	Wimplefish	*Heniochus acuminatus*	8" (20 cm)	Indo-west Pacific
31	**Golden Jacks**	***Gnathanodon speciosus***	**44" (111.7 cm)**	**Indo-Pacific**
	Almaco Jacks	*Seriola rivoliana*	28" (71 cm)	Circumglobal
	Yellowhead Jawfish	*Opistognathus aurifrons*	4" (10 cm)	W. Atlantic
32	**Kūpīpī (Blackspot Sergeant)**	***Abudefduf sordidus***	**9" (23 cm)**	**Indo-Pacific**
	Tinker's Butterflyfish	*Chaetodon tinkeri*	7" (18 cm)	Hawai'ian Islands
	Kikākapu/Ornate Butterflyfish	*Chaetodon ornatissimus*	8" (20 cm)	Central & West Pacific

H (at row 28)
I (at row 30)
J (at row 31)
K (at row 32)

33 HAWAI'IAN ENDEMIC FISHES (MARKED WITH *) AND SPECIES PARTICULARLY ABUNDANT THERE:

*Lau wiliwili/Milletseed Butterflyfish	*Chaetodon miliaris*	6½" (16.5 cm)	Hawai'ian Islands
*Kikākapu/Multiband Butterflyfish	*Chaetodon multicinctus*	4¾" (12 cm)	Hawai'ian Islands
*Kikākapu/Bluestripe Butterflyfish	*Chaetodon fremblii*	6" (15 cm)	Hawai'ian Islands
*'Ō'ili 'uwi'uwi/Fantail Filefish	*Pervagor spilosoma*	7⅛" (18 cm)	Hawai'ian Islands
*Chocolate-dip Chromis	*Chromis hanui*	3½" (9 cm)	Hawai'ian Islands
*Potter's Angelfish	*Centropyge potteri*	5" (12.7 cm)	Hawai'ian Islands
*Bandit Angelfish	*Desmoholacanthus arcuatus*	7" (18 cm)	Hawai'ian Islands
Lau'ipala/Yellow Tang	*Zebrasoma flavescens*	8" (20 cm)	Hawai'ian Islands, W. Pacific
Humuhumu nukunuku apua'a/ Reef or Picasso Triggerfish	*Rhinecanthus rectangulus*	10" (25 cm)	Indo-Pacific
*Lauia/Regal Parrotfish	*Scarus dubius*	14" (35.6 cm)	Hawai'ian Islands
*Flame Wrasse	*Cirrhilabrus jordani*	4" (10 cm)	Hawai'ian Islands
*Psychedelic Wrasse	*Anampses chrysocephalus*	7" (18 cm)	Hawai'ian Islands
*Laenihi/Blackside Razorfish	*Xyrichtys umbrilatus*	9" (23 cm)	Hawai'ian Islands

L

34	**Scribbled Leatherjacket**	***Aluterus scriptus***	**28" (71 cm)**	**Tropical & Subtropical Seas**
	Horseshoe Leatherjacket	*Meuschenia hippocrepis*	9½" (24 cm)	Indo-west Pacific, Australia
	Pygmy Leatherjacket	*Brachaluteres jacksonianus*	1⅝" (3.5 cm)	Indo-west Pacific, Australia
	Peacock Lionfish	*Pterois volitans*	12" (30 cm)	Indo-central Pacific, Australia
	Graceful Lizardfish	*Saurida gracilis*	8" (20 cm)	Indo-central Pacific

M

35	**Highfin Moray & Cleaner Wrasse**	***Gymnothorax flavimarginatus***	**20" (50 cm)**	**Indo-Pacific, Australia, S.E. Asia**
	Mandarinfish	***Synchiropus splendidus***	**2¼" (6 cm)**	**W. Pacific, Australia**
	Tropical (or Pearly) Moray	*Gymnothorax margaritophorus*	16" (40.6 cm)	Indo-west Pacific
	Harlequin Crab	*Lissocarcinus laevis*	3½" (8 cm)	Indo-Pacific

36	**Manta Ray**	***Manta birostris***	**width to 22' (6.7 m)**	**Tropical & Temperate Seas**
	Clarion Angelfish	*Holacanthus clarionensis*	to 8" (20 cm)	E. Pacific, Sea of Cortez
	Remora	*Remora remora*	15¾" (40 cm)	Circumglobal
	Whitemouth Moray	*Gymnothorax meleagris*	40" (100 cm)	Indo-Pacific
	Marine Betta (Comet)	*Calloplesiops altivelis*	6½" (16 cm)	Indo-west Pacific, S.E. Asia

N

38	**Needlefish**	***Strongylura strongylura***	**18" (45.7 cm)**	**Indo-west Pacific, Queensland**
	Reef Needlefish	*Strongylura incisa*	40" (101.6 cm)	Indo-west Pacific, Great Barrier Reef
	Chambered Nautilus	*Nautilus pompilius*	to 8" (20 cm)	Indo-Pacific

O	39	**Ocean Sunfish**	*Mola mola*	120" (305 cm)	**Circumtropical**
		Common Reef Octopus	*Octopus cyanea*	16" (40.6 cm)	Indo-Pacific

P	40	**Princess Parrotfish**	*Scarus taeniopterus*	13" (33 cm)	**W. Atlantic, Bermuda to Brazil**
		Sipadan Parrotfish	*Scarus sp.*	10" (25 cm)	Sipadan
		Egghead Parrotfish	*Scarus oviceps*	9" (23 cm)	West & Central Pacific
		Palenose Parrotfish	*Scarus psittacus*	11" (28 cm)	Indo-Pacific
	41	Greenblotch Parrotfish	*Sparisoma atomarium*	4" (10 cm)	W. Atlantic, Florida to Caribbean
		Bicolor Parrotfish	*Cetoscarus bicolor*	24" (60.5 cm)	Red Sea to W. Pacific

Q	42	**Queen Triggerfish**	*Balistes vetula*	20" (50.8 cm)	**W. Atlantic, Massachusetts to Brazil**
		Queen Angelfish	*Holacanthus ciliaris*	12" (30 cm)	W. Atlantic, Bahamas to Brazil
		Queen Coris (Red-tailed Wrasse)	*Coris frerei (formosa)*	16" (40.6 cm)	W. Indian Ocean

R	43	**Rainbow Wrasse**	*Coris gaimard*	15" (38 cm)	**Indo-central Pacific, Hawai'i**
		Green Razorfish	*Xyrichtys splendens*	5" (13 cm)	Bahamas, Caribbean to Brazil
		Masked Rabbitfish	*Siganus puellus*	9" (23 cm)	W. Pacific
		Bluespotted Sting Ray	*Dasyatis kuhlii*	30" (76.2 cm)	Indo-west Pacific

S	44	**Dusky Squirrelfish**	*Sargocentrum vexillarius*	7" (17.8 cm)	**Bermuda, Florida, Bahamas, Caribbean**
		Blackbar Soldierfish	*Myripristis jacobus*	8¼" (21 cm)	W. Atlantic, Bermuda to Brazil
		Schoolmaster	*Lutjanus apodus*	25" (63.5 cm)	W. Atlantic, Bahamas to Brazil
		Mutton Snapper	*Lutjanus analis*	31" (78.7 cm)	W. Atlantic, Massachusetts to Brazil
		Copper Sweeper	*Pempheris schomburgki*	5½" (14 cm)	Bermuda, Caribbean to Brazil
		Blacktip Shark	*Carcharhinus limbatus*	100" (254 cm)	Temperate & Tropical Seas
		Reef Shark	*Carcharhinus perezi*	120" (300 cm)	W. Atlantic, Bermuda to Brazil
		Squirrelfish	*Holocentrus adscensionis*	12" (30 cm)	W. Atlantic, Bermuda to Brazil
	47	Harlequin Sweetlips & juvenile	*Plectorhinchus chaetodontoides*	20" (50.8 cm)	Indo-west Pacific, S.E. Asia, Australia
		Oriental Sweetlips & juvenile	*Plectorhinchus orientalis*	18" (45.7 cm)	Indo-west Pacific, S.E. Asia
		Sea Slug (Nudibranch)	*Hexabranchus sanguineus*	4" (10 cm)	Indo-Pacific
		Paddletail (or Humpback) Snapper	*Lutjanus gibbus*	20" (50.8 cm)	Indo-central Pacific, S.E. Asia, Australia
		Checkered Snapper	*Lutjanus decussatus*	12" (30 cm)	S.E. Asia, Indo-Australian Archipelago
		Flametail Snapper	*Lutjanus fulvus*	16" (40.6 cm)	Indo-central Pacific, S.E. Asia, Australia
		Whitetip Shark	*Triaenodon obesus*	85" (216 cm)	Indo-east Pacific
		Tassled Scorpionfish	*Scorpaenopsis oxycephalus*	12" (30 cm)	Indo-central Pacific

Starry Moray	*Echidna nebulosa*	28" (71 cm)	Indo-east Pacific
Bluelined Surgeonfish	*Acanthurus lineatus*	13" (33 cm)	Indo-central Pacific, S.E. Asia, Australia
Orangeband Surgeonfish	*Acanthurus olivaceous*	14" (35.6 cm)	Indo-central Pacific, S.E. Asia, Australia
Shrimpfish (Razorfish)	*Aeoliscus strigatus*	6" (15 cm)	Indo-west Pacific, S.E. Asia, Australia

T 48 **Regal (or Palette) Tang**

Regal (or Palette) Tang	*Paracanthurus hepatus*	**12" (30 cm)**	**Indo-west Pacific**
Achilles Tang	*Acanthurus achilles*	12" (30 cm)	Central & East Pacific, Hawai'i
Whitecheek Tang	*Acanthurus nigricans*	8" (20 cm)	Indo-Pacific
Convict Tang	*Acanthurus triostegus*	10" (25 cm)	Indo-Pacific
Lavender Tang	*Acanthurus nigrofuscus*	6" (15 cm)	W. Pacific to Hawai'i

49

Clown Triggerfish	*Balistoides conspicillum*	10" (25 cm)	Indo-Pacific
Picasso Triggerfish	*Rhinecanthus aculeatus*	7¾" (20 cm)	Indo-Pacific, Hawai'i
Blue & Gold Triggerfish	*Pseudobalistes fuscus*	12" (30 cm)	Indo-Pacific, Red Sea
Trumpetfish	*Aulostomus chinensis*	25" (63.5 cm)	Indo-Pacific
Goldmann's Sweetlips	*Plectorhincus goldmanni*	24" (61 cm)	W. Pacific & Palau

U 50 **Bluespine Unicornfish**

Bluespine Unicornfish	*Naso unicornis*	**27" (68.6 cm)**	**Indo-Pacific, Red Sea**
Vlaming's Unicornfish	*Naso vlamingii*	20" (50.8 cm)	Indo-Pacific
Orangespine Unicornfish	*Naso lituratus*	12" (30 cm)	Indo-Pacific, Red Sea, Hawai'i
Spotted Unicornfish	*Naso brevirostris*	20" (50 cm)	Indo-Pacific

V 51

Spotted Velvetfish	*Caracanthus maculatus*	**2" (5 cm)**	**Indo-central Pacific**
Velvet Sea Star	*Echinaster luzonicus*	**7" (18 cm)**	**W. Pacific, Australia**
Madagascar Velvetfish	*Caracanthus madagascarensis*	2" (5 cm)	Madagascar
Pygmy Coral Croucher	*Caracanthus unipinna*	1⅛" (2.9 cm)	Indo-west Pacific
Blue Star	*Lincka laevigata*	12" (30 cm)	Indo-west Pacific
Crown-of-Thorns Starfish	*Acanthaster planci*	12" (30 cm)	W. Pacific to Mexico, Galapagos

W 52 WRASSES OF THE GREAT BARRIER REEF:

Chiseltooth Wrasse	*Pseudodax moluccanus*	10" (25 cm)	Great Barrier Reef, Indo-Pacific
Bi-color Cleaner Wrasse	*Labroides bicolor*	5½" (14 cm)	Great Barrier Reef, Indo-Pacific
Southern Tubelip	*Labropsis australis*	4" (10.2 cm)	Great Barrier Reef, Indo-west Pacific
Diana's Hogfish	*Bodianus diana*	10" (25 cm)	Great Barrier Reef, Indo-west Pacific
Lyretail Hogfish	*Bodianus anthioides*	8¼" (21 cm)	Great Barrier Reef, Indo-Pacific
Black-spotted Wrasse	*Macropharyngodon meleagris*	6" (15 cm)	Great Barrier Reef, Indo-west Pacific
Goldstripe Wrasse	*Halichoeres hartzfeldii*	8" (20 cm)	Great Barrier Reef, Indo-west Pacific

Redbreasted Maori Wrasse	*Cheilinus fasciatus*	14½" (36.8 cm)	Great Barrier Reef, E. Africa, Red Sea
Dusky Wrasse	*Halichoeres marginatus*	6¾" (17 cm)	Great Barrier Reef, Indo-Pacific
Ocellated Wrasse	*Halichoeres melasmapomus*	5½" (14 cm)	Great Barrier Reef, Indo-Pacific
Feminine Wrasse	*Anampses femininus*	9½" (24 cm)	Great Barrier Reef, S. Pacific
Spotted Wrasse	*Anampses meleagrides*	8¼" (21 cm)	Great Barrier Reef, Indo-west Pacific
Violet-lined Maori Wrasse	*Oxycheilinus diagrammus*	12" (30 cm)	Great Barrier Reef, Indo-west Pacific
Breastspot Cleaner Wrasse	*Labroides pectoralis*	3¼" (8 cm)	Great Barrier Reef, Micronesia, Coral Sea

53	**Moon Wrasse**	***Thalassoma lunare***	**12" (30 cm)**	**Indo-Pacific**
	Bird Wrasse	***Gomphosus varius***	**11" (28 cm)**	**W. Pacific**
	Checkerboard Wrasse	***Halichoeres hortulanus***	**10⅝" (27 cm)**	**Great Barrier Reef, Indo-Pacific**
	Bi-color Cleaner Wrasse	***Labroides bicolor***	**5½" (14 cm)**	**Great Barrier Reef, Indo-Pacific**
	Sunset Wrasse	*Thalassoma lutescens*	12" (30 cm)	Indo-Pacific
	Peacock Wrasse	*Cirrhilabrus temmincki*	4" (10 cm)	W. Pacific, S.E. Asia, Australia
	Clown Coris, female & juvenile	*Coris aygula*	to 24" (61 cm)	Indo-Pacific, Red Sea

54	Chameleon Wrasse	*Halichoeres dispilus*	8" (20 cm)	Indo-Pacific, Galapagos
	Bluehead Wrasse	*Thalassoma bifasciatum*	6" (15 cm)	Caribbean, S. Florida, Bahamas
	Three-lined Wrasse	*Stethojulis strigiventer*	6" (15 cm)	Micronesia, Samoa to E. Africa

55	Harlequin Tuskfish	*Choerodon fasciatus*	12" (30 cm)	W. Pacific
	Dragon (or Rockmover) Wrasse	*Novaculichthys taeniorus*	10" (25 cm)	Indo-Pacific
	Exquisite Wrasse	*Cirrhilabrus exquisitus*	3¼" (8 cm)	Indo-Pacific
	Slingjaw Wrasse	*Epibulus insidiator*	12" (30 cm)	Indo-Pacific
	Napoleonfish (Humphead Wrasse)	*Cheilinus undulatus*	92" (237.7 cm)	Indo-Pacific

X	56	*Xiphasia setifer* (Hair-tailed Blenny)	*Xiphasia setifer*	20" (50 cm)	**Red Sea to W. Pacific**
		Redfin Anthias	*Pseudanthias dispar*	3¾" (9.5 cm)	W. Pacific, Australia
		Flashlightfish	*Photoblepharon palpebratus*	3½" (9 cm)	Central & West Pacific, Great Barrier Reef

Y	57	**Yellowhead Butterflyfish**	***Chaetodon xanthocephalus***	**8" (20 cm)**	**E. Africa, Indian Ocean**
		Lemon Coral Goby	***Gobiodon citrinus***	**2" (5 cm)**	**Red Sea, Indo-west Pacific, Australia**
		Golden Damselfish	*Amblyglyphidodon aureus*	4¾" (12 cm)	Indo-west Pacific, Australia
		Pajama Nudibranch	*Chromodoris quadricolor*	2" (5 cm)	Red Sea (endemic)
		Purple-spotted Nudibranch	*Chromodoris kuniei*	2⅜" (6 cm)	Indo-Australian Archipelago, W. Pacific
		Red-tailed Triggerfish	*Xanthichthys mento*	9½" (24 cm)	Indo-Pacific, including Galapagos
		Caribbean Reef Squid	*Sepioteuthis sepioidea*	12" (30 cm)	Florida, Bahamas, Caribbean

ACKNOWLEDGMENTS

Fishes have been swimming through my life for many years. They made their way into this book through the kindness of both friends and strangers: Cathy Drew, whose enthusiasm for my first set of stamps led to their publication by The River Project; the Postmaster of Palau, for his forbearance in approving stamps of their fishes blithely delivering mail; Paul Gottlieb of Abrams, whose uncanny intuition spawned this book; and "Smitty," C. Lavett Smith, curator emeritus of the American Museum of Natural History, New York, who blessed me, from the first fish, with his encouragement, vast knowledge, and deep love of fishes. He saved me from some painful errors; those that remain are my own.

My deepest respect and gratitude go to all the fish lovers, scientists and nonscientists alike, whose work on the reefs has produced a tidal wave of new knowledge about the lives of the fishes. Their writings are a bottomless sea of information from which I drew the material for the text. Many of these authors are also photographers, and to them I owe a special debt. They have been my eyes underwater, their beautiful and revealing images of fish behavior are the source of many illustrations. From so many I can name only a few: Gerald Allen and Roger Steene, prolific authorities on Pacific fauna; David Doubilet and Douglas Faulkner, poet-photographers and defenders of the reefs; Paul Humann on the fishes of the Caribbean and the Galapagos; Robert Myers for Micronesian fishes; the venerable Jack Randall, my final authority on almost any question; Carl Roessler, Jeremy Stafford-Deitsch, Michael Wong, Norbert Wu, and many, many others. Thanks also to Dave Behrens for guiding me through the world of invertebrates, and to Mark Heckman of the Waikiki Aquarium for unraveling the intricacies of Hawai'ian fish names. My special thanks to Roberta and James Wilson, authors of *Watching Fishes: Understanding Coral Reef Fish Behavior*; it is the essential book for the rest of us. Thanks also to my editor, Julia Gaviria, scrupulous and patient, for helping me to actually finish this book. And a grateful bow to my sister, Elizabeth Bixby, who endured my underwater obsession while providing an untroubled place to work—and three squares a day.

Finally I must thank the fishes themselves, and honor their coral world, so essential to the balance of nature. Sadly, this beautiful world is in grave danger. Dense coastal development, marine and inland pollution, overfishing, and rising water temperatures have already destroyed a tenth of the world's reefs. More than half the rest are at risk. Sylvia Earle, the renowned marine biologist, says that the greatest threat to the ocean is ignorance. Perhaps to learn about the wonderful world of the fishes is to see the urgent need to change our own.

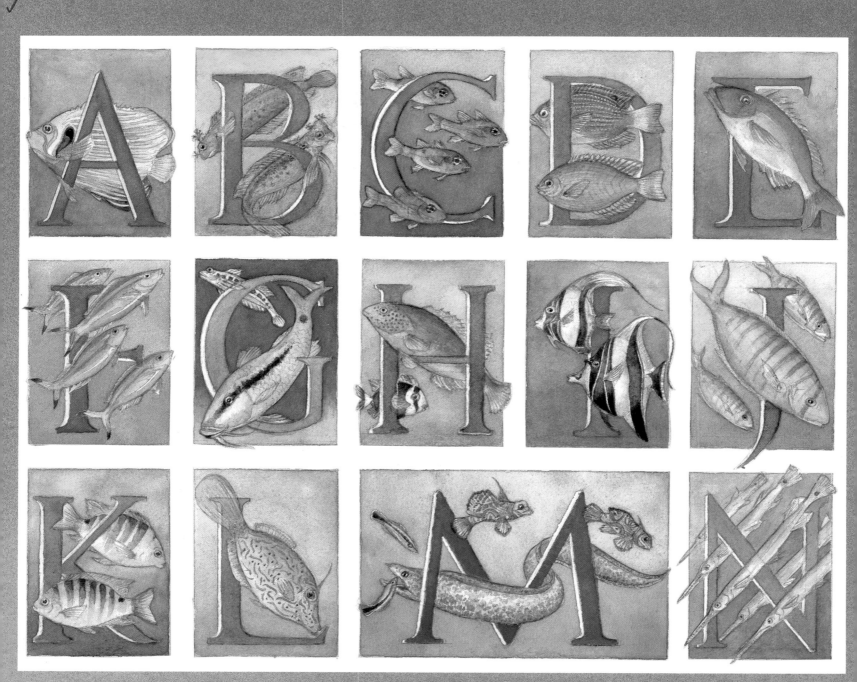